Establishing and maintaining a Christian home is the greatest contribution a man will make in a lifetime.

Love is more than dreams. Love is a manner of life . . . that which causes people to develop healthy attitudes toward themselves and toward others.

How to Succeed in Family Living emphasizes the value of the family unit and the home in God's plan.

HOW TO
SUCCEED IN
FAMILY LIVING

BY CLYDE M. NARRAMORE

A Division of G/L Publications
Glendale, California, U.S.A.

Quotations from **The Amplified Bible** published by Zondervan Publishing House, and from **Good News for Modern Man** published by the American Bible Society, used by permission. Quote of Dwight L. Moody from **Halley's Bible Handbook** published by Henry H. Halley, used by permission.

Published by
Regal Books Division, G/L Publications
Glendale, California, U.S.A.

Library of Congress Catalog Card No. 67-31425

CONTENTS

Chapter 1

GOD'S PLAN
FOR FAMILY SUCCESS

*And be ye kind one to another, tenderheart-
ed, forgiving one another, even as God for
Christ's sake hath forgiven you.*

Ephesians 4:32.

I was enjoying what we have come to call
gracious living." I was seated at the dinner
table with this obviously successful business man
and his wife and three lovely children. As the
meal progressed and we got into conversation I
became increasingly impressed. Here indeed was
one of the most remarkable men it has ever been
my privilege to meet. He was brilliant and had
real insight!

"No wonder he's such a success in his field," I
remarked to myself. As I stretched out and relaxed in the living room after dinner, I really
looked forward to a delightful chat with him.

Interested in his family, I channeled the con-

1

versation in this direction and asked him about his children.

Never will I forget the change in this man. To this day I can see him. He looked as though he were a thousand miles away.

Never have I met a man who was so much a tiny child as far as having any understanding of his own family. No interest whatever!

How could he? I kept asking myself. How could this "business giant" be completely disinterested in his family relationships? He was so gifted, so brilliant, filled with insight into everything else we had discussed. He had outstanding abilities that made him the success he was. Yet in this particular he registered almost zero.

I sat in that attractive living room almost unbelieving.

From outside came the sound of children playing. They, too, claimed my attention. Were their homes the same as this one? Did the fathers in their homes have the same attitude? Had the vital importance of their home occurred to any of them? They may have been business successes, yes. But business is structured on the home and the family. The home is the vital unit of society. God so ordained and planned and patterned it. On the home depends the church, business, schools, government, even the nation itself!

The establishing of a great family is the most important, far-reaching accomplishment in the world. It is far greater than designing the Golden Gate or Verrazano Narrows Bridge, far greater than composing "Silent Night," or painting "The Last Supper." A great family is "big business."

Establishing and maintaining a Christian home is the greatest contribution a man will make in a lifetime. And my host had never discovered this truth. His wife had. I could sense the warm feeling that existed between the children and their mother. But it's a mistaken idea that this is solely and wholly the job of the mother.

The all-important emotional climate of the home is set by both parents. This "emotional climate" is a feeling that can be sensed by persons in the home. It is something each can feel between himself and the others in the family. And this is the factor that will determine whether children will grow up to be well-adjusted individuals or maladjusted, problem-laden teenagers and adults. This is what will shape their entire lives. Oh, if we could only shout this from the housetops!

When the father in the home does not recognize his privileges and responsibilities before God, the "emotional climate" suffers. Whatever the obvious material advantages his children enjoy—even with a mother who shows them much love and affection—they will be compensating for the lack of fatherly involvement.

Another couple, Jim and Alice Alden, wrote: "Dr. Narramore, we've heard you on the radio and we would like to ask if you can suggest some kind of test we could give ourselves. We want our home to have the 'right emotional climate' you talk about."

This is good. That was a good letter. Here is a young couple, realizing the vital importance of what I've been saying in these last few paragraphs. They had determined, "If the kind of home our kids grow up in is all that important, then we'd better get with it. We don't have that much time. We'd better evaluate ourselves as parents and, if we find we need to improve (and who doesn't?), we better do something about it."

In this letter I could sense an honesty, a real desire to measure up to what God expects of parents to whom he has given this most responsible of all tasks: bringing up a child to know, love and serve him.

Of course our first responsibility is to God. We have to see ourselves in his mirror, the Bible.

In Jeremiah 17:9 (Amplified Bible) we read, "The heart is deceitful above all things, and it is exceedingly perverse and corrupt and severely, mortally sick!" When we realize this truth we are far less prone to think of our marriage partner as being the "one wrong" in any situation.

When Christ comes into our lives he gives us a new set of values. This is the basis of true self-analysis.

Accepting Christ is the foundation for understanding our own human tendencies. As we take him at his word and are truthful with God, we become truthful with ourselves.

A good marriage has to have these elements of truth and honesty. Periodic check-ups, rating sheets and self-evaluation tests, can often be helpful in uncovering hidden motives and feelings.

Here is the test we recommended to the young couple who asked for one. See how you rate!

FOR HUSBANDS

1. Do you allow your wife an appropriate

amount of the family income to spend as she chooses, without accounting?

2. Do you still "court" her with an occasional gift of flowers: by remembrances of birthdays and anniversaries; by unexpected attentions?

3. Are you cooperative in handling the children, taking your full share of responsibility and also backing her up?

4. Do you make it a point never to criticize her before others?

5. Do you share much of your recreation hours with her?

6. Do you show interest in and encourage her to develop intellectually?

7. Do you show as much consideration for and courtesy to her relatives as you do your own?

8. Do you enter sympathetically into her plans for social activities, trying to do your full share as a host in your own home? And when you are a guest in the homes of others, do you try to make her appear to the best possible advantage?

9. Do you make an effort to understand the peculiarities of feminine psychology and to help her through her varying moods?

10. Do you tell her at least once a day that you love her, and act as though you meant it?

11. Do you give spiritual leadership to your family?

12. Do you encourage your wife to talk things out?

FOR WIVES

1. Do you try to make the home interesting, attractive, cheerful, a place of rest and relaxation? Do you devote as much thought and study

to that as you would a job "downtown"?

2. Do you encourage your husband to spend some time with his men friends?

3. Do you serve meals that are enticing in variety and attractiveness?

4. Do you handle household finances in a businesslike way?

5. Do you keep yourself attractive in appearance so that your husband may be proud to have everyone know you are his wife?

6. Are you a good sport: cheerful and uncomplaining, punctual, not nagging, not insisting on having your own way or the last word, not making a fuss over trifles or requiring your husband to solve minor problems that you should handle alone?

7. Do you bolster your husband's ego, not comparing him unfavorably with more successful men but making him feel that he is successful?

8. Do you prevent your mother and other relatives from intruding unduly, and show courtesy and consideration to his relatives?

9. Do you take a sympathetic and intelligent interest in his business?

10. Do you cultivate an interest in his friends and recreations so you can be a satisfactory partner in his leisure activities?

11. Do you talk things through with him?

12. Do you encourage your husband and your children in the things of the Lord?

By your testing of your own actions and attitudes, you are in a sense praying the sage prayer of Scotland's Robbie Burns:

"O wad some pow'r the giftie gie us
    To see oorsels as ithers see us."

Socrates likewise believed the great achievement was to "know thyself." But in itself is this enough?

I'm sure you will agree with me that it is not enough just to get a "weather report" on the climate in our marriage and in our home. The only justification for finding out "what goes" is (like the couple who wrote for the test) so that we can do something about it.

If an honest evaluation has revealed a need for improvement, then the next question should be, "What am I going to do about it?"

Since God instituted marriage and the home, he is the one who knows all about it. He is the ultimate "Marriage Counselor." One of Christ's names given in Isaiah 9:6 is "Counselor."

He places the Bible in our hands not only as a road map to point us to heaven, but as a manual of behavior while we're on our way to heaven.

God ordained that couples should be happy, and he prescribed the formula for happiness.

I know of a pastor who never permits a couple to leave the altar on their wedding day without first sharing with them this formula: "And become useful and helpful and kind to one another, tenderhearted (compassionate, understanding, loving-hearted), forgiving one another [readily and freely], as God in Christ forgave you" (Ephesians 4:32, Amplified Bible). Now that verse gives a code that if heeded and practiced, is guaranteed to assure a wonderful measure of success in family living.

Chapter 2

EMOTIONAL CLIMATE

In this life we have three great lasting qualities—faith, hope and love. But the greatest of them is love. I Corinthians 13:13, Phillips.

The young Bensons had scarcely unpacked after the honeymoon before they began to have little disagreements.

"Betty! You're positively the most stubborn person I've ever met," accused George.

"Well, I'm not half as stubborn as you," Betty defended herself, "George Benson, you're the most bullheaded person in all the world."

"Little disagreements" developed into young giants.

Month after month and year after year their problems nagged them. Several times Betty suggested they go to a marriage counselor. "Why? What can he do?" asked her husband. "If you weren't so stubborn everything would be all right. Why go and pay someone to tell you something you already know?"

Many couples are like the Bensons. If they were suffering from an illness or injury they would not hesitate to call a physician, recognizing that the medical profession is trained to treat their physical ills. But unfortunately, when it comes to an ailing marriage or family difficulties and problems, they would rather let the relationship deteriorate and finally die than seek professional help.

What kind of emotional climate are they creating for each other—and for their three children? How will this climate affect all five of them?

Another couple, Bob and Marla, were also having trouble. No matter what Bob said, Marla was certain to construe it as criticism. His marriage was like walking on light bulbs. He had to be so careful—too careful.

The longer they were married the more Bob resented her attitude. Then one night he read in a magazine about a similar case except that it was the man whose feelings were always getting hurt. Even so, the symptoms were clearly like Marla's. He could see her on every page. But not only did he read about the symptoms. He read about the causes: certain experiences in childhood and during the teen years had created this ultrasensitiveness. Bob realized his wife had never resolved these feelings. In fact, she didn't understand how serious her behavior was—to say nothing about its causes.

Armed with this insight and understanding, Bob's own attitude changed. He encouraged his wife and began to lead her into talking about some of her earlier experiences. A strict father and critical grandmother had raised her. She had no mother to whom she could turn. Other experiences in adolescence with several teachers and a youth director had affected her deeply. Sharp tongues and critical attitudes of childhood had made Marla feel especially vulnerable to criticism. In time, however, through patience as well as through discussion of her feelings, Bob was able to help his wife to a measure of self-understanding. He, in turn, could now accept the fact that Marla's reactions were not directed toward him but rather they were a natural reaction to childhood and teen-age experiences.

For the Christian, there is the blessing of God-given insight as well as the help of trained counselors.

Many a couple could benefit by the experiences of the Bensons as well as those of Bob and Marla.

Another undeniably strong factor that affects a person's attitudes is the "guilt complex"—a phrase coined in our day—but guilt feelings are as old as human history, and, completely universal.

The late Sir Arthur Conan Doyle used to tell with rare glee a practical joke he had played on his friends. According to the story, he sent a telegram to twelve famous people, all of whom were men of great virtue and reputation: men of considerable position in society. The message was worded, "Fly at once, all is discovered."

Within twenty-four hours all twelve of the so-called virtuous men had left the country! Husbands, wives—yes, and children who do not confess their sins and live in close communion with God, suffer from feelings of guilt. Many families would be much happier if they learned to humbly admit their sinful attitudes and behavior, and ask Christ to forgive them. But so often they refuse to do so, thereby living in an atmosphere of anger, quick tempers, criticism and a host of other carnal traits.

The majority of us try to camouflage or rationalize our guilt, but we strongly suspect that the guilt is still there. Ever since the beginning, when Adam and Eve used their free will to choose evil, the conflict has been good versus evil, innocence versus guilt.

Book shelves and magazine racks bulge with treatises and articles about the "guilt complex." This guilt complex is standard equipment for all human beings, whoever or wherever we may be. "For all have sinned, and come short of the glory of God" (Romans 3:23).

What happens when we continually feel guilty? How does it affect our health and personality?

It robs us of our happiness because it's a nagging reminder that we have not done the right thing.

It shatters our confidence. We look into ourselves and see our own imperfections. We're weak—and we know it.

Guilt feelings remind us of the past and dim our future. Like Adam and Eve we want to run and hide from God.

The total result? We may feel insecure, hostile, defeated, critical, unworthy.

How incisive is the Word of God when it declares, "But the wicked are like the troubled sea, when it cannot rest. . . . There is no peace, saith my God, to the wicked" (Isaiah 57:20,21).

"We must do something about this," insists the psychologist and psychiatrist. "Find ways to erase the guilt complex from people's minds."

In our day besides "resolving" and "rationalizing," discounting sins as mere human "mistakes," counselors too often lead their clients to think of sin as a behavior pattern which has not yet been incorporated into our society—"frowned upon here" but "acceptable there."

Sounds nice? Yes. But—IT DOESN'T WORK. Man does not have the power to remove sin.

We smile as we watch our children at play. When our Melodie was just a little girl, it amused us to see her play "hide and seek," for, when it was her turn to hide, it made little difference to her if she were completely hidden or not. Just so her face was hidden so that she could not see us, she seemed to think neither could we see her.

But are we any better in our reasoning, many times?

We cannot hide from God. And we're deceiving nobody but ourselves. "If we say that we have no sin, we deceive ourselves ... but if we confess our sins to God, we can trust him, for he does what is right—he will forgive us our sins and make us clean from all our wrongdoing" (I John 1:8,9, "Good News for Modern Man"). Here is real freedom—God's freedom from secular, worldly attitudes.

It's not only adults who have emotional problems. Any casual observation of children and young people will impress you with the great varieties of emotional problems which plague them. For example, today it is believed that many children as well as adults are suffering from depression. In a child this can exhibit itself in such ways as low grades in school, despite above average intelligence.

Sometimes serious feelings develop because of the loss of a parent by separation, divorce, death or lack of mutual emotional response.

Good emotional and mental health may be defined as a dynamic balance amid the stresses and strains of life.

Today, after working in this field for years and now directing clinics where we offer more than two thousand hours of professional counseling each month, I have learned that no one is emotionally healthy all of the time. We have our "highs" and our "lows." These can materially affect the household climate.

Often, all it takes to lower the temperature to a comfortable degree is as simple a thing as Christian love and appreciation shown to one another.

A young lady poetess, after going the rounds of publishers, finally got the ear of an editor.

"So you have some poetry you would like me to put in my magazine," he queried. "What's it about?"

"All about love," she answered.

"Hmmmm," the editor mumbled, "Well, tell me, what is love?"

Soulfully the poetess began, "Love is filling one's soul with the beauties of the night, by the shimmering moonbeams on the lily pond when . . ."

"Stop! Stop!" cried the editor. "You are all wrong—very, very wrong. I'll tell you what love is. It's getting up cheerfully out of a warm bed in

14

the middle of the night to fill hot water bottles for a sick child. That's real love. I'm sorry, but I don't think we can use your poems."

The editor was right. Love is more than fanciful dreams. Love is a manner of life—that which causes people to develop healthy attitudes toward themselves and toward others.

The "love chapter" of the Bible, I Corinthians 13, is one of the most practical sections of the entire New Testament. It's about feeding the poor, and having right attitudes towards our fellow men. Not a word about moonbeams! It's all about the kind of love that will keep our family life at the right temperature, the emotional climate God intended it should be.

Chapter 3

HOUSEHOLD BAROMETER

Love one another with brotherly affection—
as members of one family—giving precedence
and showing honor to one another.
> Romans 12:10, Amplified Bible.

"Climate-controlled." It's a big word in business these days. It sells refrigerators, apartments and automobiles, among other things. There is, however, another kind of "climate" that subtly regulates. It has an infinitely greater and far-reaching effect on our lives.

So, when Joe Brown folds himself into his compact car, frowns a bit, backs out the driveway and heads for the freeway, he mutters, "I guess it's the weather." He can't explain his feeling even to himself. It could indeed be that Joe is stating a known fact: There is an element of "weather" or emotional climate that registers on the household barometer.

There had been somewhat of a storm at the breakfast table. Young Joe and his father had had a difference of opinion. Joe pushed on the pedal as he grumbled aloud, remembering, "Used to be he would listen and take his dad's advice. But now—"

"Dad, why do you think you have to be right *all the time?*" With his mouth half-full of Wheaties, he had gone on, "Don't you suppose that maybe *I* could just possibly be right—*this one time?*"

Jane had meant well but it hadn't helped when she chipped in, "Why, Son! That's no way to talk to your father."

Later, when his blood pressure had gone down a bit, Mr. Brown thought over the breakfast situation. Sitting in his office, he admitted to himself, "Maybe the kid has something. I guess I jumped on him too fast."

Joe was proving what we have stated earlier, "No one is emotionally healthy all of the time." And a compulsion to "be right" triggers household storms.

How many marriages have floundered on this very thing? "Having to be right," chipping away at each other as though proving which one is right would alter the course of world history! Usually it's a trivial, non-consequential fact that starts this, but it is a storm signal nevertheless. It is the warning of worse weather ahead unless the signs are heeded and something is done about it.

"In honor preferring one another" (Romans 12:10). In fact the entire verse holds the key to clearing the air: "Love one another with brotherly affection—as members of one family—giving precedence and showing honor to one another."

18

No room here for arrogance—"being right" all the time.

And this "preferring one another" means more than "letting your wife go through a revolving door on your push," as someone has aptly put it. It means being unselfish enough—and big enough —to say, "Honey, I could be *wrong* about that."

Ten chances to one, she will say, "Oh, no! Of course you're right. I guess I was being impatient."

A good jumping off place for a healthy marriage is the realization by both husband and wife that marriage involves two fallible human beings.

Another factor that can set the household barometer at a steady low is the practice of "playing favorites."

They were brothers. Sons of a father whose name would become world-renowned. One was an outdoor boy; the other a kind of stay-at-home fellow. They were twins.

The father set great store by his young hunter son. The mother centered all her affection on his brother. She was bound that "her boy" would fall heir to all his father's belongings and the rights that went with these.

That is a capsuled setting for the Bible's classic story of favoritism. You can read it in Genesis 27.

What a time modern newsmen could have with this! A scheming mother—a half-blind, sick-unto-death (as they thought then) father— weak-willed son—an underhanded plot to deceive the father—an enraged brother declaring murderous revenge.

What benefit did either conniving Rebekah or

equally-blameworthy Jacob get out of this? The son had to run for his life and it's an open question whether Rebekah ever again laid eyes on her favorite son.

We all know cases of family favoritism.

Joanne's parents habitually compared her—always unfavorably—with her older sister. "Why can't you get A's like Andrea does?" The poor girl heard it all the time.

This has the effect of making a child feel unworthy, rejected and will create a hurdle for her to jump all the rest of her life.

Then there's Steve. He could never please his parents, either. His younger brother could play ball better—run track faster—do everything so much better, that Steve developed a "Why should I bother to try; it won't work anyway" attitude.

The extent to which this type of treatment from parents can affect a person in later life is shown in the case of Lois, a foreign missionary.

In our Counseling Clinic we offer special help to missionaries and their families and Lois was one who came after a term of service on the mission field. She had experienced some difficulties while there, and now, at home, she was suffering physical ailments as well. In the course of counseling with her and with her husband, it became evident that Lois's problems stemmed from nothing less than the feelings of rejection, left over from childhood days in a home where her sister had been the favorite. Her whole childhood and adolescence had been marred by this awareness. Now as a young woman, the scars remained. For, as the twig is bent, so grows the tree. Even in the case of a servant of the Lord:

saved, committed to Christ—yet having child-hood problems still unresolved.

No home is ever likely to escape problems of one kind or another. We can be sure of this. But, if there is one element that can tend more than almost any other to swing the household barometer to "Fair and rising," surely it is communication.

How much misunderstanding would never be allowed to cloud the home if fathers and mothers, children too, would only talk things out.

"Silence is golden" we're told. But there are times when silence is *not* golden. In order for human beings to relate to and understand each other, they must be able to talk things over. One of the biggest roadblocks to marital happiness is lack of communication. It can lead to misunderstandings, suspicion, quarreling and divorce. At the best, it leads to a miserable marriage.

Helen and Roy had been married for some time, but the years had been cloudy ones. Helen frustrated over her husband's unwillingness to discuss family problems with her. Roy responded to her outbursts of anger with an icy, "You women are funny. You just want to talk about everything all the time. I'll take care of my business and you take care of yours." By what standard was family business *not* "his business"? Helen would counter with a derogatory remark, and the fight was on.

Makes me think of a story I heard. A true one, at that! A couple were married in their church but without all the trimmings of a "formal church wedding." At the close of the ceremony, the organist who was waiting for the choir to appear for rehearsal remarked, "What piece would you like me to play?"

Quick as a flash the witty bride called over her shoulder, "Just play 'The Fight Is On.' "

But family fights are nothing to joke about.

The fact is that Roy did not know what it meant to talk things over. His parents and his brothers and sisters had never shared their feelings or their doings. They were "independent." The result was that Roy had never learned to communicate with others. Not only did he keep things to himself that he should have shared with Helen, but he refused to work out their marital problems by discussing them with her. Thus tension and resentment was created on both sides.

The art of talking things over is the oil that keeps a marriage running smoothly. When this oil is lacking, there are bound to be some rough places: rubbing each other the wrong way; grating on each other.

When this "oil" is the oil of the Holy Spirit; when Christ is invited to be present—how blest and profitable is this "talking it over."

Discussion relieves tension. When this door is closed tensions mount high. Talking is like an escape valve.

Many common problems will respond to this non-pill therapy.

The approach can make worlds of difference. For instance, ask yourself, how would I react to either of these two responses?

1) "How absurd! Mother isn't running our lives at all!"

2) "You feel then that Mother is interfering too much in our marriage?"

No. 1 invites argument.

No. 2 gives the husband (or wife) an opportunity to drain off any bitter feelings. In addition it makes him/her feel that there is a respect for his/her opinion.

Like every aspect of marriage, communication is something that can be cultivated. Here are a few proven pointers:

Read books or articles together. This allows communication which does not carry high emotional content.

Avoid unpleasant discussion at wrong times, such as early morning, bedtime, before dinner, when either of you is tired, or during times of stress.

Respect each other's right to express his own opinion—even if it is wrong!

Learn to listen attentively. It's not very inspirational to talk to someone who is only half listening. Also, *try not to interrupt.* Let each of you feel you always have the privilege of finishing whatever you have to say.

By learning to understand the motives behind ideas, you can more readily accept each other's attitudes.

Above all, be guided by the wisdom of the Bible. "A soft answer turneth away wrath" (Proverbs 15:1). It really does. This is not some up-in-the-air idealistic, non-workable notion. It works!

We should keep in mind that conversation—communication—when it's good, is never one-sided. Indeed, how can you discuss without both taking part? But some people have never learned the art of sharing a conversation. Instead of drawing the other person out, they dominate the conversation; never giving anybody else a chance to get a word in edgeways. This has the effect of pushing the somewhat introverted partner right into a secluded corner. What the less talkative person needs is someone to show an interest in what he or she has to say.

No husband and wife are ever going to agree about everything, but it's important that you be agreeable! It pays off in good relationships and a happy marriage.

How truly has someone said, "Deep spirituality is the glue that holds a marriage together."

This is one kind of glue that will not seal the lips but will rather unseal them at the right times.

In later chapters we'll be dealing with our teenagers in our homes and with this matter of communication. Surely a subject for volumes all on its own. But, listen to Ted, as he shares his feelings with a fellow his own age: "You say you wish your dad would quit lecturing you all the time? Me, I'd even settle for that, I guess. Just so he would say something. I never know what he's thinkin' and he sure doesn't care what goes on in my head either. He just sits."

Here is a relationship robbed for lack of communication.

Oliver Wendell Holmes wrote, "Talking is like playing on the harp. There is as much in laying the hands on the strings to stop their vibrations as in twanging them to bring out their music."

But what if the strings were never "twanged"?

How would we ever know what kind of music they are capable of producing?

Maybe strains that would make the listener feel warm and glowing all over.

Chapter 4

Eph 5- 20-33

WHO'S WHO

Wives, be subject—be submissive and adapt yourselves—to your own husbands as [a service] to the Lord. Husbands, love your wives, as Christ loved the church and gave Himself up for her.

Ephesians 5:22,25, Amplified Bible.

Listen in on the conversation of almost any group of young boys. At some point you'll hear, "My dad can pitch better'n yours."

"Boy! Can my dad make a neat model plane."

"Making pancakes? My dad's the greatest."

"Sure your dad's okay, but mine's better."

It might be any one of a dozen kinds of "great" the fellas are discussing. And incidentally, rarely will you hear, "My dad makes more money than yours."

Apparently this has doubtful "great" value on the scale of the Little League crowd.

What makes a great man?

What marks a "better dad"?

It has been said, "It takes three generations to make a great man." This may be debatable but it is a fact of history that many of our great men have had fathers and grandfathers of noble character. Men who molded the generation following them. Sons naturally emulate their fathers.

A father is intended by God to be the leader of his household; the strong figure of spiritual truth, an example of Christian character, the priest of his household who prays to God for the welfare of each one in his family.

Marriage involves both husband and wife. Each of these partners must assume his responsibility in making his marriage go. It's the man's place, however, to choose the values that go into a home. It's the man who determines whether the family will be sports-minded or book-lovers; travelers or "stay-at-homes." Likewise the man's influence will govern whether his is a family to whom personal integrity is important, or who will be clever manipulators getting along on their wits. Whether they'll be society conscious or quiet introverts. The family imprint is usually stamped there by the father in the home.

Every man is ultimately responsible to God for what his home becomes. This is the clear, unmistakable teaching of the Bible.

Listen to the apostle Paul as he makes this plain in the early days of the Christian church: "But I want you to know and realize that Christ is the head of every man, the head of a woman is her husband" (I Corinthians 11:3, Amplified Bible).

So within the framework of total leadership in the universe, God assigns to the husband leadership within the home.

Oh, I know it's popular to talk about "bossy wives." And we don't dispute the fact that there are women who dominate the situation in the home. But I would submit to you that the problem is not so much due to wives demanding to assert leadership, as it is the refusal of husbands to assume their responsibilities.

Men often give themselves to careful responsible leadership in business or their profession. Yet these same men, when they get home, may expect everything to roll along just fine and turn out right without much thought or direction or leadership on their part!

It is when the husband does not exert leadership that the wife must do so. He forces her into a role for which she is not fitted, and moreover, that she doesn't want.

Women's instinctive desire for male leadership comes through in a paragraph from an article written by a woman and addressed to husbands: "Don't yield your leadership, that's the main thing. Don't hand us the reins. We would consider this abdication on your part.... Oh, we will try to get you to give up your position as Number One in the house. (That's the terrible contradiction in us.) We'll fight you ... but in the obscure recesses of our hearts, we'll want you to win, for we aren't made for leadership. It's a pose."

An honest admission!

The father's leadership role falls into several categories including spiritual emphasis and education.

"I let my wife decide whether the children are to go to Sunday School and church. That's her department."

Such statements only reveal the lack of spiritual maturity of the husband. The father who will assume the spiritual leadership in his home is providing the needed father-image for each member of the family. In order to qualify as a successful spiritual leader, the father must be spiritual himself. He must be a born-again believer in Christ. Not only so but he must have a knowledge of the Word of God. Otherwise, how can he influence his children, lead them to a knowledge of personal salvation, and instruct them, as the Bible exhorts him to do (Eph. 6:4).

This portion of Scripture places an educational responsibility squarely on the shoulders of every father. Every member of a family is an intellectual being. This distinguishes him from the animal world. Each person is designed to accomplish something in God's eternal plan. A happy family is one that is learning and developing. It is up to the father to stimulate his family and provide them with opportunities for learning.

There never was a day when so much enrichment can be provided—reading, films, music, hobbies, trips, home projects—all these add up to the satisfaction of hearing Junior brag to his friends, "My dad's the best dad in the whole world."

There will be times when he doesn't think so.

When you have to exercise your father's authority in the area of discipline. This, too, is what God expects of a father who would honor him. What is discipline?* It is a way of life that helps children to grow up to love the Lord, to gradually control themselves, and to develop positive attitudes toward themselves and toward others.

* See the author's book, *Discipline in the Christian Home,* published by Zondervan.

The Bible gives us pictures of ideal fathers: neither dictators nor weak-willed, hot-tempered nor indecisive, hardhearted nor irresponsible.

Love for children is shown by careful, patient instruction and by kind, thoughtful, sympathetic discipline which regards the child as a person with feelings.

A good father sets the example of the type of character he wishes to develop in his household, and seasons the whole with affectionate, firm and impartial love.

To be appreciated, love must be shown as well as felt. There's Mr. Jones, for instance. A well-meaning father, but like so many others, so preoccupied with his work that he has scarcely an hour to enjoy his family. Someone asked him, "Do you really love your family?"

He was indignant. "Of course I do. Love them? Why else d'you think I slave like I do—all the long hours—I just don't have time to play games with them, that's all."

If he could just have heard Harriet, his oldest teenager say, "Yes, Dad works hard and sees to it that we're well provided for, but somehow I feel something's missing. I never feel that I really have a dad."

Meanwhile, Father is reading all this and saying to himself, "Hey! When am I supposed to be doing all this? You'd have me running 'junior church,' a hobby shop, taking educational trips and all that."

You're right! It is Mom's place to keep the home a restful, relaxed place for you to come home to. That's why she needs your cooperation.

"Duty" and "beauty." These spell the main areas of the wife and mother's role. And this is

'Bible spelling": "In the same way you wives must submit yourselves to your husbands. . . . Your beauty should consist of your true inner self, the ageless beauty of a gentle and quiet spirit" (I Peter 3:1,4, "Good News for Modern Man").

Here we have the duty of a wife, and the beauty of a woman. And no matter how often a woman may read the Bible, or in which particular version or translation, it always comes out the same. God's Word says, "Submit."

This is by no means a tyrant-slave relationship, and the necessity of the wife to submit herself to her husband's authority becomes a source of joy to a wife who is well adjusted.

No leader can go farther than his followers will permit him. So it's only as the wife is willing to permit and even to encourage her husband to lead, that he is able to fulfill the role God has assigned him.*

"Being in subjection to her husband" is also necessary if a woman is to be a woman. The masculine feminist with her mannish suit and gravelly voice is a sad caricature of what God intended a woman should be. And what man is impressed with her?

"My lord and master" some women say and with, all too often, sheer sarcasm. It's interesting to note that when Sarah used the term of respect to her husband, Abraham, it was her idea, not his! (See Genesis 18:12.) What a wonderful woman she was! So strikingly beautiful that even at the age of sixty she was taken by Pharaoh of Egypt for his harem (Genesis 12:11,14,15). More

---

* These concepts are highlighted in Ray Steadmor's booklet, "What Every Wife Should Know," published by the Narramore Christian Foundation, Rosemead, California.

amazing still, this episode was repeated when Sarah was ninety years old! (See Genesis 20:2.)

But Sarah's fame in the New Testament (I Peter 3:6) doesn't rest on her physical beauty. It rests on her beauty of spirit. And was ever a wife so mourned at her death? (Read Genesis 23:2.)

Abraham is one of the great names in Scripture. In fact, one of the few men known all over the earth. How great a part, we might well ask, did his wife, Sarah, play?

Fred's wife asked him to fix the screen door. He fully intended to do it but a day or so went by and he didn't have an opportunity. His wife interpreted this as willful reluctance and launched a nagging campaign. After two days Fred decided, "I'll show her. I'll never fix the old screen!" He finally let it fall off its hinges where it lay for weeks. Cathy, his wife, was outraged. What a way for a man to act!

But, in truth, although we can't condone Fred's attitude, the key to it lay in his wife's nagging threat to his leadership.

Cathy would have spent her time more profitably if, after the initial request, she had left the matter with Fred. A quiet spirit, the "inner beauty" would unquestionably have accomplished more. "You catch more flies with honey than with vinegar" is true in other realms than "fly-catching."

Personal attractiveness is part of a woman's duty to her husband and family.

Keeping her home attractive: pleasant to come home to, with an air of warmth whatever the temperature. A place guests can feel at home in. Where members of the family can bring their friends knowing the welcome mat is out and the door swings in. Where meals are well-planned and attractively served. Where through some organization such as a worker in an office is expected to maintain, the mother in the home gets her work done and still keeps from having that "I've been slaving over a hot stove all day" look when her family arrives home for dinner.

She may not be the paragon painted by Solomon in Proverbs 31: spinning and sewing and accomplishing an amazing amount of work, but by this "Looking well to the ways of her household," she will know the joy of "her children calling her blessed"—and without a doubt, her husband will praise her.

What a challenge to women in every age!

Then there are the areas where husband and wife function as partners.

A Bible teacher once explained, "God did not take a rib from Adam's head so that he would 'lord it over' Eve.

"God didn't take a rib from Adam's feet so that he would trample her underfoot.

"God took a rib from Adam's side that the two might walk side by side: partners."

Neither can be wholly dominant in everything in marriage, for in the blending of two lives, there is fashioned one new life.

There's one area where this partnership cooperation is crucial. That's in the discipline of the children. How many of them have been caused to become emotional wrecks, or spoiled brats, or both, because of a situation like this, repeated many times:

Janice screams at her child, "Just you wait till your daddy comes home! You'll. . . . "

So Daddy comes home to be greeted with, "Am I glad to see you, Tom! I've been telling Buddy he'd get it when you got home. What a day I've had with him."

"Now look here, Honey, I'll not be a policeman to my son. After all, I'm gone all day. Surely you can handle him." And Tom picks Buddy up, ruffles his hair a bit, plays with him. To Buddy this spells approval. Mommy hates him. Daddy loves him.

Time the partners got together. Did some communicating. Set up a few ground rules, before Buddy becomes hopelessly confused, and his values jell in the wrong mold.

Another home scene. Paul comes home and toddler Jeff waddles to meet him. The table is set. The high chair drawn up next to Paul's place at the head of the table. It's like a ritual, this business of Daddy looking after small son Jeff at dinner time. They both look forward to it. And somehow this tall dad, executive in his profession, never looks quite so tall as when he's working with his partner, taking his share of responsibility for his little boy.

Husband and wife talk over the doings of the day; they plan for the evening and for other days ahead of them. In all of it, one word never comes through: "mine" or "me"; it's "ours" and "us."

The fortunate children in this home can tell you "Who's who." It's no problem for them to discern. Dad and Mom, of course.

John 15:1-7

Chapter 5

BOOK AT THE TOP

The word of God, which liveth and abideth forever. I Peter 1:23.

All Jane could ever remember about a Bible in her home was a large, ornately covered volume that lay on a table underneath a potted plant. The Bible was "too sacred" to be opened.

Jane's son Billy, visiting next door, was horrified when he noticed a Bible lying open and some of the verses underlined and notes in the margin.

"Goodness!" he exclaimed, "what a way to treat a Bible!"

To this family, the Bible was a closed topic. No doubt about that. It was revered, respected—and left unopened. The very special book in their home had never spoken a word to mother or son. What did they know about its being a living book?

You and I can ask ourselves, how meaningful is my Bible to me? How important a place does the Bible occupy in our home? And why the Bible? Why not Shakespeare or some other classic literature? What makes any book significant? Unique?

The author. Second, the purpose and content of the book. We have no difficulty with the authorship of the Bible. The apostle Peter makes it clear "Holy men of God spake as they were moved by the Holy Ghost" (II Peter 1:21).

The stated purpose and intent: "All scripture is given by inspiration of God, and is profitable for doctrine, for reproof, for correction, for instruction in righteousness" (II Timothy 3:16). Furthermore, said John in his Gospel, "These are written, that ye might believe that Jesus is the Christ, the Son of God; and that believing ye might have life through his name" (John 20:31). Was ever a nobler purpose set forth?

Now let's take the purpose apart. Profitable for what? In the Christian home the Bible should occupy the supreme place. It is profitable: as the basis for every decision that affects the family. Each member needs to be Bible-taught so that he can be in a position to profit by its clear teaching. Questions arise. Which college shall Tom or Mary attend? Which vocation? This should be decided according to the principles set forth in the Bible. We know there are numerous cases on record of young people having come unscathed through secular schools and colleges. This often depends on the home and church background. But it is true that I have never received a letter stating, "How we regret it that we sent our son/daughter to a Christian college." Yet scarcely a week goes by that we don't receive laments from parents whose children have attended secular institutions of learning and have become spiritual blobs or wrecks.

God should be at the very center of education. He created science and math and the atom and the anatomy of man. Indeed, that secular education is off center without God being given his rightful place.

How can we help young people make important decisions? How can they receive guidance as to the life partner they should choose, unless the Bible is paramount in the home? Bible study has to be an integral part of life, if our families are to grow up to be strong in the faith, maintaining a dynamic balance amid the stress and strains of modern life.

It's going to take more than an "instant breakfast" kind of acquaintance with the Scriptures. Reading a verse or two in the morning, and feeling we have fortified ourselves spiritually for the day we face, is not enough.

In order for the Bible to be the dynamic that motivates our thinking and governs our actions, obviously it has to become a part of us. It must be assimilated into our thinking pattern. Dwight L. Moody learned this and admitted, "I prayed for faith, and thought that some day faith would come down and strike me like lightning. But faith did not seem to come. One day I read in the tenth chapter of Romans, 'Faith cometh by hearing, and hearing by the Word of God.' I had closed my Bible and prayed for faith. I now opened my Bible and began to study and faith has been growing ever since."

One may complain, "But there's so much I can't understand, and the language is difficult and different." Not any more. That excuse doesn't hold water. For just a little looking around in a Christian bookstore, you'll be rewarded with attractive editions the whole family can enjoy and profit from. Children's Bibles, especially geared to make the Bible come alive for little folk. Modern English editions, the answer to those who object to archaic thee's and thou's.

Just a word about these new versions. If you are not sure which to purchase, ask the advice of a pastor.

We like the cadences of the King James. The majesty of the old English, but there is nothing sacred about this particular edition of the year 1611. For the now generation in our homes, the vital aim is that they know the truth of the Bible.

Parents must not assume that the schools will take the responsibility of teaching the Bible to their children. This is "homework" for parent and child alike.

God leaves no alternative. His Word is clear on this (Deuteronomy 6:6,7). Family devotions is at the very heart of this Christian training. We can imagine that as the Lord looks down on us, it rejoices his heart to see a family gathered around his precious Word: worshiping, praying, and learning about him.

"When is the best time for our family devotions?" we're frequently asked. While morning sets a fine pattern for the day, evening often finds families with more time to spend together. This has to be worked out by each family. What is most important is the setting aside of a regular time and sticking to it. Oh, there will be interruptions and if you heed them all, Satan will see to it that no time is the right time for you.

Some folks seem to have difficulty in knowing just how to go about establishing a family altar and conducting regular worship in the home.* For maximum interest and profit the whole family should participate. Let's take a look at the Jarmans, for example: There is Mother and Dad, Ben and Roy, teenagers, and four-year-old Susan. And each has some part.

Father should lead the devotional period. Sometimes he may ask the boys to select the Scripture to be read that day and direct the family. Mother chooses a hymn or chorus and also takes care of family prayer requests. Little Susan has the task of handing out the Bibles and devotional guide when they are used.

Singing sets a mood for worship. While a verse that was read might elude you through the day, often the words of a hymn will linger with blessing all through the busy hours.

Who can measure the value of prayer as a family is circled in petition before their heavenly Father? Requests are jotted down and just as carefully checked off when the answer comes.

No one will ever tell the members of this family that God is dead or that, as someone put it recently, "If God is not dead then he just doesn't want to get involved." Ben and Roy and little sister Susan, Mom and Dad Jarman all can testify that God is very much alive. Even little

* You may wish to use the author's book, "How to Begin and Improve Family Devotions," published by Zondervan Publishing House, Grand Rapids, Michigan.

children acquire a consciousness that prayer is the answer to problems.

One part of family devotions that will pay large dividends for a lifetime is memorizing verses. This is done more easily as the family tries together. One verse is learned. Two. Three. A dozen. Soon a workable amount of Scripture is at your disposal.

Unlike other material we commit to memory, Bible memorizing carries with it a promise. "Thy word have I hid in mine heart, that I might not sin against thee" (Psalm 119:11). But first we have to be taught by him.

It's the Word of God, the Holy Spirit uses in our lives, to guide, to comfort, to keep us from temptation.

The Word is the sword of the Spirit and if we're going to get anywhere as Christ's soldiers, we should better learn how to use it.

It's a fact that everyone is going to grow up to be devoted to something. We will never do anything else for our children that will so count, as to encourage them to become soulwinners. Each one in the family should be active in some form of soulwinning. Knowing salvation verses and where to locate them in the Bible is a prime requisite in leading someone to Christ. One family teaches their children, "Though we may move and have a different address some day, the Bible verses always stay in the same place. So learn their 'street and number' as well as the verses themselves."

Not only so, but the children should be instructed in how to use their knowledge.

A father was walking through the school grounds one day at recess. He noticed his son with a buddy backed up to a corner. Seeing his father, the boy called, "Hey, Dad! C'm 'ere. Rog is so stupid. Can you tell him how he can get to be a Christian?"

No, the boy wasn't stupid. The son was eager to lead his friend to Jesus, but he didn't know how.

For almost every infraction, Gary was sent to his room with the command, "You sit down and learn (the number according to the offence) Bible verses and be sure you really know them before you come back downstairs." Scripture should not be used to continually frighten children or to punish them.

While we would deplore Bible study or memory work as a punitive measure, certainly there is much to be gained from individual study. The adult needs more than the shared experience of family devotions. It's after a quiet time of communion with the Lord—after speaking to him and letting him speak to us—that we really have something to bring, something to share with each other in our family worship.

Teenagers will gain from the reading of devotional material geared for their own age and interests. This can often be the guide needed for systematic study that is so profitable. Sometimes taking a word, or a Bible character, or a topic and tracing it through the Bible with the help of a concordance, stimulates personal study and provides interesting "sharing" together.

I think I can hear, "This is all very fine, but in our family, it wouldn't work. You see my wife (or my husband) is not a believer. We can never have time for prayer and Bible study in our house."

41

This, sadly, is a universal problem and perhaps these few do's and don'ts will help you.

Don't make false pretenses before your mate. Live your Christianity. A consistent, godly life will speak for itself.

Don't insist on your mate having devotions with you. This may have the effect of driving him/her *away* instead of closer.

Do show you love your marriage partner regardless of his or her belief.

Do remember that your unsaved mate may not be interested in spiritual matters. The Bible reminds us, "The natural man receiveth not the things of the Spirit of God" (I Corinthians 2:14). Kindness and patience should be shown regardless of differences in viewpoint.

Do continue to carry on your own private devotions.

Do ask the Lord for appropriate opportunity to talk with your mate about the Lord. Perhaps your testimony will lead him or her to a saving knowledge of Jesus Christ.

Do keep in mind that all of us are different. There will be times when an unsaved person will appreciate brevity in the devotional period. On the other hand one should be sensitive to opportunities to explain what you are reading from the Bible. No doubt you will have to plan for additional time for your own study.

Everybody gains through regular family devotions. Besides the security, the inner awareness that God is our loving heavenly Father and that he is with us constantly—with the youngsters as they start out for school—with Dad as he may have to face temptation, or make important decisions—with the teenagers in their special need of wisdom and strength and courage to witness for him—with the mother in the home—there is also the fund of knowledge to be gained as we know better what God says.

An outstanding Christian leader once said, "I have observed that a child of twelve or fourteen who has taken part in family devotions all his life, usually knows more about the Scriptures and more about godly living than others who have not had family devotions, even though they may be seminary graduates."

When parents have been faithful in living for Christ and teaching his Word at home, they need not fear when their children go out into the world to assume their responsibilities. With Christ in their hearts, and the Bible as their guide, they are indeed happy and fortunate.

Benefits of family worship will be assured if Father and Mother are faithful and prayerful. Our Lord has promised to be present where two or three are gathered in his name. He assures us his Spirit and his Word abiding in our hearts will bear spiritual fruit through the years.

The great patriot Patrick Henry would agree. He said, "The Bible is worth all other books that have ever been printed."

The Bible's place is "at the top."

Chapter 6

WHERE THE ACTION IS

*Set your minds and keep them set on what
is above—the higher things—not on the things
that are on the earth.*

Colossians 3:2, Amplified Bible.

After her very first day in junior high, Joyce
returned home with a newly acquired air.

"What's the matter, dear," asked her mother,
"you're acting so strange?"

"Well," Joyce answered, with a toss of her long
hair, "Can't you tell, I'm completely different!"

We smile at this. But we might better sit up
and take notice, for we are being served notice
that the brand new junior high miss is changing.
She's becoming a person in her own right. This
transition calls for understanding, if not accept-
ance.

The teenager is one whose life patterns are
about to "jell," but if we hurry he is still capable

of being molded. This lends the sense of urgency to dealing with him. The teenager we don't reach today is all too likely to be out of reach tomorrow. Life patterns are taking form today. Tomorrow, the "cement may have hardened."

Life commitments are being made now. History does not reveal its alternatives. This we should admit. But who would venture to guess the difference in world history if the bookish young Indian students, Gandhi and Nehru, had been reached with the gospel of Jesus Christ when they were teenagers studying in England? Joseph Stalin and Mikoyan likewise were once students in nominal Christian seminaries. "What happened?" we ask.

"A teenager is a bundle of possibilities," the late Dr. Henrietta Mears delighted to repeat.

The business of changing possibilities into probabilities rests in the home, with the parents.

Families should normally grow and develop together. There is the difference between "getting" older and "growing" older. Anybody can "get", growing is a little harder. Growing calls for planning and providing interests.

It has been said that you are what you read. If reading does play such a major part in shaping persons, what an opportunity today's parents have. Never has there been such an array of fine Christian books and magazines. In addition to subscribing for the family, invest in one or two subscriptions for your teen-age boy or girl. This will pay off in a number of ways. They'll be gratified to get a magazine addressed to them personally. This will add importance as they read. Also, in the stories and pictures they will find that there are many others like themselves.

It may be that your growing youngster is isolated. Your church doesn't have many young people. In the magazine, he'll find Christians with whom he can identify: his "peer" group.

This is the day of the missionary biography. Not only can a father or mother point away back to the distinguished David Livingstone and Hudson Taylor, but also he can provide daring tales of the '50s and '60s. The martyrs and heroes provide idealistic teenagers with contemporary challenge.

Here, perhaps, is the answer to the plea of mission board directors. Before Isaiah ever uttered his "Here am I; send me" (Isaiah 6:8), he had been challenged by the Lord's call, "Whom shall I send, and who will go for us?" Before the five American martyrs gave their lives for Christ in Aucaland, they had first heard the call of God. Before Dr. Paul Carlson was martyred in Congo, he, too, had heard the call.

We're prone to quote, "Remember now thy Creator in the days of thy youth" (Ecclesiastes 12:1), but how can our young people "remember" what they have perhaps never heard! So—books and magazines of worth should be a part of our Christian homes.

And don't overlook Christian fiction. It, too, has its place and can have practical value for your teenagers and for every member of the family.

Christian writers, like any others, draw their material from real life around them and the real problems Christians have to face. In a well-written story, the hero or heroine must face up to his problem and find the best solution. This can often help the reader to do the same.

One Christian couple told of the impact a book made on their daughter. "Barbara was getting difficult to live with," said her father. "Then we bought her a copy of a Christian teen-age book. One of the chapters dealt with this very problem of getting along with parents. There was a distinct difference in Barbara, a noticeable change in her behavior. Evidently the author had been able to point out to her some things that she would not accept from us."

Books on dating, sex education, etiquette and Christian living can all have an important part in shaping the thinking of your teenagers.

What about music? If you were to ask a hundred persons to close their eyes, think of the word "teenager" and tell you their first thoughts, a high percentage of them would say something like this: "A bunch of writhing, wriggling creatures, motivated by an off beat thing they call 'music.' "

Music is a powerful agent—for good or for evil.

Music invades the mind simultaneously from four directions: melody, harmony, rhythm and words.

The Bible is filled with references to music, and we are admonished to "sing praises unto the Lord." This being so, we had better not leave all the "music appreciation" instruction to the schools. It's part of our responsibility to help our teenagers, in particular, to discriminate between the suitable and unsuitable, in music. As consistent Christians, we can't close our ears and allow inappropriate music to dominate our home through radio, TV, or recordings. While pointing out the negative—that much of today's so-called "music" is not honoring to the Lord—we should be sure our young people are exposed to fine gospel music.

Lorrie was one girl who "couldn't wait" to hear the next new number on the "Top Ten." Her dad stepped into her room one evening after dinner. She was "studying" with a record player going full blast on the latest popular number. She dashed and turned down the volume. Her dad nodded his approval. Later she confessed, "Daddy! If you had blasted me for having that record on. . . . But you didn't. It's not my record, I borrowed it. I'll give it back. I guess it's not much, is it?"

The Martin home was plagued by the same problem. A plaque above the fireplace promised, "Thou wilt keep him in perfect peace, whose mind is stayed on thee" (Isaiah 26:3). But from Carol's room boomed the latest rock 'n roll.

A half-hour went by. Mr. Martin put down his paper and glared over at his wife. "I'm getting fed up with this degrading racket," he exploded. "How long are we supposed to put up with this 'junk' in our own home?"

Into his daughter's room he stormed, demanding, "Stop that horrible noise!"

Feeling very much abused and misunderstood, Carol sulked off to bed.

There are many young people, and adults too, who do not realize the direct correlation between a musical diet and spiritual growth. "What difference does it make?" they ask. "We like this kind of music."

It's not a matter of liking and not liking, and it does make a difference. "We tend to live on the level of the music we listen to" is the slogan of a well-known gospel recording company.

There's nothing like a good sing around the piano on a Sunday evening after church. Nothing is more rewarding than this "do-it-yourself" music.

There are so many fine gospel artists available to us on records. We can have a personalized "sacred concert" whenever we feel like it.

We Americans are so conscious of atmosphere in the home, color harmony, wall-to-wall carpets and so forth. Yet do we recognize the value of music in helping to create a desirable home atmosphere, and in influencing thought? G. Stanley Hall has said, "For the average youth, there is probably no other agent for educating the heart to love God, home, country and for cadencing the whole emotional nature, as music."

Not just Christians appreciate gospel music. A family camping in a state park invited their Sunday School adult class to a campfire sing. So greatly did the other campers in the area enjoy the soft, melodious music that they asked when the group would be coming back to sing again.

While not everyone is musical, in the accepted sense, we all have some abilities that often just need to be cultivated or developed.

Art Williams was one of these. Art was a rug salesman. His real interest, however, was in his young adult Sunday School class. Because he had some background in psychology and knew his Bible well, his students would come to him for counsel. Also, in the course of his teaching he would sometimes discuss the significance of Christian living to good mental and emotional health.

The pastor suggested one day that Art should

set down some of this material in writing, then submit it to a magazine so that other people might benefit from it. At first Art was reluctant, but he followed his pastor's suggestion. It took more than one try but Art was no quitter, and after a couple of rejections and some rewriting, he sold his article. As he progressed he had little difficulty in getting other articles accepted. Not only did he grow himself, but others reaped the benefit of his growth.

Then there's Marie. Her life was getting stagnant now that her children were grown up and in homes of their own. She heard about some night classes for adult education in her area. Looking over the prospectus, she decided she should take typing lessons.

"Typing comes in handy lots of times," she told herself. But her eye was really on another course, painting. All her life Marie had had a secret urge, a desire she would hardly admit even to herself, to try painting. She talked this over with the admissions head of the evening school. "Why not take a try at both," was his suggestion. Marie did, and while she gained a measure of proficiency on the typewriter, it was the art course that thrilled her. Hers was no Rembrandt, but she did a creditable job of a landscape.

Before long, her paintings were adorning not only her own home, but she was sharing them with others. Through this experience Marie seemed to blossom in a new way.

Some projects lend themselves to whole family participation. The Bartons moved to a new home with a large backyard that stretched like a miniature mountain. Almost immediately Mom decided, "What we need is to terrace the yard." Little did she think what she was starting. The boys, Bill and Steve, got as excited as their mother. Dad started a compost pile as his share. Many a trip the family had to areas where they could find wild growth that was just right. Rocks and stones took on new significance for them. Proudly Mrs. Barton would show off a new plant or garden ornament to her friends. "The boys bought it with their allowance," she would beam, "for a surprise for me."

The Barton's garden became more than a "thing of beauty." It was a center of family enjoyment. Something that together they had accomplished. And in the doing of it, new under-standings of each other had come about. One had one idea, another had a different, and some "giving up" had to be exhibited.

Some of the character of each was planted in that garden. Some days the temptation of the ol' swimmin' hole beckoned. The day much of the hard work was undone by a sudden rain squall that drove the soil all downhill was a bad one. Oh, it was much more than a nicely terraced backyard the Barton family had developed.

There is a "growing" that develops only the best in any of us. "Continue to grow in the grace and knowledge of our Lord and Savior Jesus Christ" (II Peter 3:18, "Good News for Modern Man"). Those are the last words of the apostle Peter to us. No, actually the next phrase is Peter's final word and it is the "punch line": "To him be the glory, now and for ever! Amen." Isn't this what we should be striving for?

All we hear these days about "the importance of the person." All our efforts to expand our areas of knowledge. All the reading. All the listening to fine music, and feasting our eyes on great art. Nothing compares with offering of praise to Christ.

Unless we grow in grace—and how else can we do this but by increasing our knowledge of Christ—our growth might well be called "stunted."

How vital then that our young people in particular catch a glimpse of what it is to live for the glory of God, before self glory captivates them. Or the glory of a wrong cause blinds them to true values. Remember young people are idealists. Thoreau said, "If you have built castles in the air, your work need not be lost; that is where they should be. Now put foundations under them."

Dad and Mom! They'll need your help to do it!

Chapter 7

DO'S AND DON'TS

*Blessed—happy, fortunate [to be envied]—is
the man whom You discipline and instruct,
O Lord.* Psalm 94:12, Amplified Bible.

Discipline is a fighting word in some circles of
our society today. In others, concerned parents
and educators give time and thought to the
problem.

"Strict—or permissive?"

"Can we be too strict—too permissive?"

The "experts" change their minds all too frequently. What is "the proven method" this
month may be outdated by "Statistics show
that . . ." next month.

Surely we must believe that God would never
launch families and then leave parents to drift
without any compass to guide them in bringing
up their families.

The Bible gives us plenty of instruction, and it's the only "proven method"; moreover, it doesn't change.

We read, for instance, about Eli the priest of God whose sons were a disgrace to him and an abomination unto God. The explanation of this? The Bible makes it clear the father "restrained them not" (I Samuel 3:13).

This was over a thousand years before Christ, but it has a modern ring to it.

There are good reasons for "restraining," for rules, and perhaps not all parents take the time to explain this.

Jimmy hears "Don't do that!" for the twentieth time in one morning. To himself he mutters, "When I'm big, nobody's gonna tell me 'don't.' I'll do everything I want to. I'll be just like Daddy. He can do what he wants."

Many children do believe that rules are made just for them. Grownups have no such restraints, they think. This is the time to point out that everyone has to obey rules. A simple way to show this is to point out the "cross only at the crosswalk" sign or the big STOP that makes Daddy and Mommy bring the car to a halt. Teach your children that parents have to obey the civic laws. And that everyone—grownups and children alike—have to obey God's laws.

We should teach our children to respect others. They will never learn the "Golden Rule" any younger! This is not only a cardinal commandment from God and thus to be obeyed, but it is also a necessity in being able to relate to others socially. Psychologists find that one of the major areas of disturbance in mental illness is a person's inability to respect and be sensitive to the needs of others.

Mrs. Smith appeals in tears to the psychologist during an interview: "My son is terrible! I give him everything, but he seems to have no respect or love for me. He's disrespectful, has temper tantrums. What can I do?"

It became apparent that this mother considered being able to discipline her child a monumental task. The child had to learn to give and take. He had to be taught how to get along with other children. He would have to be taught that his teacher had to be obeyed.

Our children should also be taught to respect property, both at home and outside. It takes time to teach a child what is his and what is not. "Mine" seems to be a word a child learns early!

Show the child what does belong to him. Give him a place to put it and let him know it will be undisturbed. You'll find that when his property rights are respected, he will be much more willing to respect others.

Not only in the matter of property but in the general area of living, there are disciplines—for adults as well as for children. Crowded living conditions in many neighborhoods bring families almost into each other's living rooms. Johnny needs to be helped to realize that while he may have the right to yell and shout at play, the neighbor has a right to reasonable freedom from bedlam.

In spite of all we might think or hear to the contrary, children are happiest when they have the guidelines of discipline. We need to keep in mind that we are dealing with members of the human race. As such, they need guidance and control.

Many instances have proved that teenagers respect the parent who sets boundaries of behavior for them.

One girl revealed that she loved her mother, "But I don't respect her," she added. "I asked permission to hold an all-night, mixed slumber party at home without a chaperone. Mom phoned some of the other mothers to see how they would handle the request."

Deploring "parental indecision" and "do-nothing" attitudes, psychologists would tell this girl's mother that her daughter wanted her to say a firm "No!" The girl didn't want to have the party but couldn't stand the loss of popularity if she herself declined. This mother didn't know her own daughter.

One of the most important things a parent can do is spend time with his child. It's easy, I know, with our busy schedules, appointment-filled days, to say "I don't have time." The time given to our children is spent, invested, not squandered. It's from your contact with your son, walking with him, talking to him, finding out the things that are important to him, that he learns a sense of self-importance. And Dad learns to understand his boy and what makes him tick.

While we must be true to the scriptural injunction and apply correction when it's called for, we should try to understand the reason for the child's behavior. The child is immature. He has no vast store of experiences to determine his choices, so quite often he will do things that the mature adult will not understand. It's not always a matter of willful disobedience.

When it is "beyond reasonable doubt" that punishment is in order, mete it out. All our lives we learn through punishment. If, in a temper tantrum, Mary breaks her favorite toy, she'll learn she has punished herself. Denied a privilege because of disobedience, Kevin will think twice before he disobeys again.

"You wouldn't spank, Dr. Narramore," some folks have suggested to me, "not in our civilized society."

Oh, no? There are times when spanking is a very effective means of discipline.

"The rod and reproof give wisdom: but a child left to himself bringeth his mother to shame. Correct thy son, and he shall give thee rest; yea, he shall give delight unto thy soul" (Proverbs 29:15,17).

Whatever the means used—and understanding of your own child will determine this in each case—one fact stands out, the child must be made to feel he is still loved by his parents, even though they disapprove of a particular action and have to punish him for this.

Some parents try to buy their children's love. Does this sound unreasonable? It's quite often true. Mrs. Smith tried to shower her son with material things in order to win his love. It was done unconsciously, of course. However, children are "perceptive little psychologists." They can often "see through" and sense that some material gifts may be given to make up for some lack on the part of the parent.

In this vein, paying a child for every household duty performed by him is not always advisable. He needs to be taught that each is a contributing member of the household, and a task performed is part of his responsibility.

There is probably nothing that challenges a

person more than responsibility. This is equally true of adults and children. For the child in the home, it not only fills up idle moments, thus keeping him out of trouble, but it makes him feel he is accepted as an important part of the family. So don't be afraid to place a reasonable amount of responsibility on your son and daughter. Remember, however, they're still children. Don't expect perfection.

Another point to remember is to avoid too much criticism. This can be most discouraging. Of course, it's natural to scold a child when he's not doing what he should, but criticism has no value because it offers no solution.

We can reduce the sting of criticism by saying, "Honey, you did part of this very well, but I think some of it could be done better, don't you?" Or, "I think you could have done better, and I'm sure you will the next time."

It's not always that our children know what we mean, or the significance of it even if they do know the words. We should prepare them for what we expect. This will get them ready emotionally to do what we expect, and to do it happily.

In one home it was the same thing every Sunday morning, for weeks. Mother: "Betty, what's the matter with you? You know this is Sunday and we have to leave for Sunday School in ten minutes. Why are you so slow?"

Four-year-old Betty: "Mommie! I didn't know it was Sunday."

There was three-year-old Brent, in the back seat of the car. A couple of times his dad had called over his shoulder, "Brent! stop that whining."

60

The third time the father said it, the child asked, "If you cry twice, is that whining, Daddy?"

Brent was willing, apparently, but what did Daddy want him to do?

In setting up "do's and don'ts" for our families it's wise to make these somewhat flexible. While rules and standards are necessary, humans are not machines. Don't be afraid to bend a little when the occasion demands. Not only will the children respect you, they'll love you all the more for understanding.

Another area that calls for understanding is when a parent must take action against a particular bit of bad behavior.

Bobby wants to tear up your favorite magazine. He clutches it in his grubby little two-year-old arms.

Try handing him his favorite red ball and watch what happens. With the teenagers, the same applies. Condemning "the wrong crowd" your son has begun to run around with will only antagonize him. Offer him the "red ball" of inviting friends into the home. Introduce him to other boys and girls his age. Talk to him as a reasoning person about the qualities that attract friends.

Making each member of the family a part of the family planning can start with even the little tots. For example, one mother lets her little girl choose from four, which dress she will wear to school the next day. Families can plan recreation and vacations. Knowing the financial limitations makes a member of the family more reasonable. Being a part of the planning, he's scarcely likely to rebel at what's decided.

In this matter of rebellion—indeed with every

phase of discipline—nothing is more important than prayer. We are spiritual beings. Prayer, like every form of child care, takes time. We might take a lesson from an experienced mother. She didn't have much time, either. Still Susanna Wesley made it a point never to let a day go by without spending some time alone with each of her children, praying with them and for them. And she had nineteen children. Among them were men of destiny. John and Charles Wesley contributed much to a religious revival that transformed England.

The single most important factor in discipline is the spiritual emphasis. Teach your child about Jesus. Be sure he is saved. Then help him to live for the Lord day by day. When you have done this, you will have obeyed God. He says, "Train up a child in the way he should go: and when he is old, he will not depart from it" (Proverbs 22:6).

What will be the advantage to your children? "All thy children shall be taught of the LORD; and great shall be the peace of thy children" (Isaiah 54:13).

Who could ask for more?

Chapter 8

DESIGN FOR ACCOMPLISHMENT

Live purposefully and worthily . . . making the very most of the time.
Ephesians 5:15,16, Amplified Bible.

"If a man's not a success by the time he's thirty-five, he'll never be one." I was quite a young boy when I heard a neighbor say this. Immediately I pricked up my ears. Not only did I swallow his statement, but I supposed "success" was spelled M-O-N-E-Y.

Years later I discovered this is not true. Oh, the neighbor hadn't been lying; he was sincere enough. He just didn't know the facts.

Actually there is no age beyond which one can say, "He'll never be successful." And contrary to popular opinion, true success has very little to do with the size of a man's bankroll.

But success and achievement are highly important. In fact they are vital to our physical and mental health. Success draws the best out of a man, and, in return, it tends to fill him with normal, healthy attitudes. The result is a well adjusted person.

Success can be called "The pay-off for our efforts." Nothing is more pitiful than the person who is standing still or going backwards.

Marie is an example of such a person. Circumstances had prevented her from finishing high school. She had to take the only job open to her in her community and with her limited education. She became a file clerk. Filing—filing—filing, and hating every minute of it.

This was not success and well Marie knew it. Naturally this was reflected in her personality. No zest—little happiness—constant conflict.

On the other hand no one is more interesting than the person who is moving forward. Man was made to move forward. As we do, we grow, we develop, we mature and our personalities take on a vibrant sparkle.

This moving forward—accomplishment we call it—always involves change.

Two psychologists were talking one day about the theory of change. "Do you know what our biggest problem is?" asked one, then proceeded to answer his own question. "Just this: as psychologists we can give examinations, study people, then come up with scientific findings. But here's the rub: we can't change people."

And this psychologist is right. We can and do help people alter their attitudes, to some degree at least. But basic changes of character and personality? Too big a job for human beings. These are for God to do. Thoroughgoing changes come only as you "Commit thy way unto the LORD" (Psalm 37:5). God made us. He can change us in ways that will be reflected in our attitudes. He can endue us with "self confidence" that is rather, trust and confidence in him. "Trust also in him; and he shall bring it to pass," the psalmist adds.

"What does 'getting right with God' have to do with confidence?" you might ask. A great deal! We can never over-estimate how much.

We have: a forgiven past,
        a clean present, and
        an optimistic future.

No one can feel confident when he is "burdened 'neath a load of sin." This knowledge of sins forgiven gives a person confidence in his relationship with God and man. Who can measure what it does to a man to realize, "For as the heaven is high above the earth, so great is his mercy toward them that fear him. As far as the east is from the west, so far hath he removed our transgressions from us" (Psalm 103:11,12)?

Confidence thrives on peace of mind. And peace, "the peace of God, which passeth all understanding," is the legacy of everyone whose trust is in Christ as personal Saviour. "Peace I leave with you," Jesus said (John 14:27). With this peace in our hearts and in our minds we can forge ahead.

The apostle Paul had a great understanding of what God expected of us. Something like this Paul would probably say to us in our generation, as we strive for success: "Don't stand still. Press on. Forget the past that would hamstring you, and reach beyond. See what God can do with you and through you in the future."

Success is the basis for greater accomplishments. Yes, it takes more than striving to develop a well adjusted personality. It takes some arriving. Success then, to some extent at least, is essential if a person is to maintain good health, both mental and emotional. Continual failure, on the other hand, can have adverse physical effects. It can upset the body's glandular balance, cause headaches, backaches and other physical ailments.

One day Mr. Burton came into my office, his face tired and haggard. His whole attitude and bearing was one of dejection and defeat. "I don't know what's the matter with me, Dr. Narramore," he confided, slumping down into a chair, "but—oh—everything seems to be wrong."

Then he told me his story. He had been a Christian for a number of years, had a fine wife and two lovely daughters. Seemed he had everything to make him happy, but yet he was miserable.

"I'm so discouraged," he confessed, "I don't want to be like this but I'm terribly unhappy. I'm just a big failure, I guess."

Here was a man who by his own admission was plain dissatisfied on the job, at home, in his church, in fact everywhere. And to him life was intolerably dull.

"I'm tired all the time, and I just don't feel well," Mr. Burton continued. "Yet when I went to our family doctor and had a complete physical check-up, he couldn't find a thing wrong. But something is wrong."

I can still hear the stress in that man's voice.

"And whatever it is, I do hope you can help

me find my trouble."

Poor health? Yes, but not from a physical cause.

As I talked with him, I soon sensed that here was a brilliant man (subsequent tests proved him to be in the "gifted" category) spending his days working at a job anybody, with almost no education, could handle. All day long, men with far less ability than he had, were giving him orders. And in his particular company there was nothing he could do about it.

Various aptitude tests uncovered the fact that Mr. Burton had special ability in several lines for which he had no training or experience. I encouraged him to start night school, and if possible, to get a leave of absence from his work so he could attend summer school at a nearby university. He did, and after two years he moved to a new company and into a position for which he had unusual talent and where he could utilize his recent training. In almost no time he gained recognition in his office and was shortly afterward promoted to a top executive position.

End of this story? Mr. Burton's poor mental health disappeared. At home, at work, in his church he was radiantly happy. Success made the difference. He had found his niche.

In many people's minds it seems the ultimate in success would be not having to work for a living. How wrong this thinking is. Work produces dignity of character.

Think! God could have so created the Garden of Eden that it never needed tending. But right at the beginning of time, Adam was put "into the garden of Eden to dress it and to keep it" (Genesis 2:15).

The first two boys in the world had their jobs, too. One a shepherd; the other a gardner/farmer.

The New Testament, likewise has something to say that would seem revolutionary to many today. "If any would not work, neither should he eat" (II Thessalonians 3:10). Naturally we are thinking of healthy, able people who could work.

Accepting a position implies, to the employer, that he is getting an employee who will be responsible, will do a good job. Of all people, Christians should be the most scrupulous in this respect.

This is practicing, "Whatever you do, work at it with all your heart, as though you were working for the Lord, and not for men ... for Christ is the real Master you serve" (Colossians 3:23,24, "Good News for Modern Man").

Good work habits are something we acquire over a lifetime, but many of them have their beginnings in how we do things at home.

How do we use our time? There are a few basic principles intelligent people can follow in order to make the most of our 1440 minutes a day. (And all of us have the same amount of time!)

A place for everything. Every item you own occupies space and it takes up as much in one place as in another. Isn't it common sense then to put it in the most convenient and meaningful place?

Keeping similar things together is a timesaver: cans of soup together, bars of soap together. All the way from "shirts and ties" to "bolts and nuts" this kind of togetherness pays off in time saved. It saves time in putting things away and it saves time finding them.

We're all familiar with this kind of home situation:

After jumping into the car, Joe Brown realizes he doesn't have his car keys. "Elizabeth!" he yells, "where are the car keys?"

"I don't know, dear. Who used the car last?"

This answer is no help. Joe runs into the house and looks on several tables. Next he tries rummaging in his dresser drawers. He shouts to his teen-age son, "Bill, do you have the car keys?"

"No, Dad, but you can use mine if you want to."

"Give them to me. I'm in a hurry," his dad answers.

Bill reaches down into his pocket, then realizes he must have left them somewhere.

"Well," says Dad grimly, "we just have to find those keys."

So, the hunt is on, and before the keys are finally located all the Browns have lost time and Dad, in particular, has almost lost his religion!

The Carsons, living next door, have a simple system. They place their keys, whenever they come into the house, in a little box in the entry closet. This saves time and avoids unpleasant emergencies. Oh, it's not perfect. They forget once in a while, but for the most part they have little trouble locating car keys.

A little time saved here. A little there. This can add up. And as Christians we have the urging of the Bible to spur us on: "Live purposefully and worthily and accurately, not as the unwise and witless, but as wise—sensible, intelligent people; making the very most of the time—buying up each opportunity" (Ephesians 5:15,16, Amplified Bible).

Filing written materials in orderly combinations need not be an elaborate process. Most stationery stores carry assortments of files: small, medium and large, to accommodate almost anything that needs to be kept where it can be readily available. This practice saves literally hours of rummaging to find those things that "I thought I could put my hand on right away!"

Preplanning not only saves time but assures a better end result. For example: Rev. Frank Dickens receives a phone call inviting him to speak at a certain function. Immediately he jots down a few thoughts on the assigned topic. He drops these into a file labeled "Engagements." From time to time he adds notes as the subject runs through his mind. When, a day or so before the presentation, he gathers these together and makes an outline for his address, he really has something to work on. He can confidently appear on the platform.

Contrast this procedure with that of Rev. Billings. He waits until the last minute to figure out what he is going to say, then practices on his audience.

The practice of making shopping lists is a mark of a well organized person. The Davises work together on this. Mrs. Davis keeps a memo pad in the kitchen and another in the bedroom. Mr. Davis has one in his office and another in the glove compartment of his car. Thus, when they go shopping, they get everything at once. This saves time and means they actually buy what they need.

Two department store clerks were discussing the customers. Said one, "I'd never make such good commission if it weren't for the impulse buying of so many of my customers." We might give some thought to this comment.

To get back to our use of time. Short cuts, if they do not spell "shortchange," are good stewardship of our time. It's the man or woman who habitually looks out for a quicker way to do the job better at home, who lands the "suggestion awards" in business. Every company is in search of efficiency, proficiency and savings.

It's a credit to the Christian who gains recognition as an outstanding workman in the office, in his position in education, manufacture, or in the arts. Not only is it personally gratifying, but he is bringing credit to the cause of Christ.

"Whatsoever thy hand findeth to do, do it with thy might," said the wise man of the Bible (Ecclesiastes 9:10). And if you try doing this often enough, first thing you know it will be a habit.

mark 6: 30-37

Chapter 9

THE FAMILY THAT PLAYS TOGETHER

A merry heart doeth good like a medicine.
                                    Proverbs 17:22.

The cliche of all cliches must surely be, "All work and no play makes Jack a dull boy." Nevertheless, even those who despise this phrase will have to admit that what made it so overworked is the very truth it expresses.

In the family realm, when for the father it's a case of all work, everybody suffers. How important it is for fathers to play with their children.

I'll always remember the time I was giving an individual intelligence test to a little boy in the first grade. After I had worked with him for a little while he looked up and said, "You know what?"

"No, what?"

73

"My daddy loves me."

"How can you tell?"

"Because"—a big grin spread over his face—
"Because he plays with me."

Simple childish reasoning. "My daddy plays
with me. My daddy loves me."

Third grade Ken was explaining to his uncle,
"My friend Tommy can't catch a ball. He fum-
bles all the time. Know what I think, Uncle
Bill?"

"What, Ken?"

"I think his daddy doesn't play with him like
our daddy plays with Bruce and Kathy and me."

Fortunate the child whose parents take time
out for family fun and games together.

A boy's confidence can be built up as he learns
proficiency in the games he's expected to be able
to play. A thoughtful father will have this in
mind as he takes time off to "toss a few balls"
with his son. Life can be cruel for the boy who
has to stand by, afraid to play because he doesn't
know how.

How often we hear, "The family that prays
together stays together." This is undeniably true.
It's equally true that "The family that plays
together stays together."

A group of older teenagers were recalling
some of the things they best liked to remember
about their growing up.

"I like to think of the times we'd leave the
supper dishes and go out and play together for a
while before dark. Sometimes we raced each
other, sometimes we played croquet or badmin-
ton. Lots of times it was 'scrub team' softball.
Mom was about as good as any of us. Lots of
times it was dark before those dishes got done."

Real, honest-to-goodness fun is priceless. It's wholesome and uplifting, and makes you a finer person. One of the secrets of happiness is the ability to have fun. And it's good for you.

God tells us, "A merry heart doeth good like a medicine" (Proverbs 17:22). This kind of "medicine" isn't hard to take, is it?

The Bible tells us to "rejoice and be glad" and to "rejoice evermore" (Psalm 40:16; I Thessalonians 5:16).

Mark Twain said, "To get the full value of joy, you must have someone to divide it with." And who better than our own family to divide it with, to share it with!

Have you ever felt like smiling a little at the person who asks, "What do Christians do for fun?"

What do we do? Why, the list is endless.

Some Christians even ask this question!

Two couples were talking along this line one evening. Said Gerry Owen: "It's okay to say we should have fun, but what is there for a Christian to do?"

His wife, Anne, spoke up. "We don't dance or go to night clubs or . . ." and she rhymed off a list of negatives. "What's left to do, either for us or our kids?"

"What's left?" exclaimed Joy Adams, "Why, everything that's worthwhile, that's what!"

How right Joy is.

Everything that's worthwhile, everything that's wholesome and uplifting, everything that leaves you feeling good afterwards. That's the kind of fun there is for a Christian. And there's plenty of it to be found.

Persons like Gerry who aren't merry because

their Christianity "limits" their fun are only re-vealing their own personal lacks. Yes, lacking in spirituality, in personality, in imagination, in ver-satility, and in Christian training.

What do I mean? Simply this. He's lacking spiritually because a person who is in close fel-lowship with the Lord will have no interest in worldly amusements. In fact such amusements will be distasteful to him. God makes it plain in the Scriptures, "Love not the world, neither the things that are in the world. If any man love the world, the love of the Father is not in him" (I John 2:15).

He's lacking in personality because a person who is alive and interesting and vital can always think of something to do—and have a good time doing it. It's usually the "drip" who doesn't know what to do with himself.

He's lacking in imagination because with all the myriad things to do, if he can't think of something, he'd better start sharpening up a little.

He's lacking in versatility because he just doesn't know how to do anything. In that case he'd better start learning, if he doesn't like being "left out."

And he is lacking in Christian training because he just doesn't know. We don't get our joy and satisfaction through the things we do. We get it through Christ and through being in God's will.

The fact Gerry needs to realize is that it's the non-Christian who has a harder time finding something to do. That's right. Much harder be-cause he tries to find satisfaction in the worldly amusements. And when it's all over, all he has is pffffff! A burst balloon. An empty shell. So he looks for something else that will provide a "kick." But that doesn't satisfy either. And he'll never find what he is looking for until he finds Christ.

What do we do?

When I was in my teens, we lived in a small community surrounded by a desert. And I loved it. To me, a desert was the most wonderful place in all the world to live. We had family picnics, weiner roasts, horseback rides, corn roasts, steak fries, parties, church doings, sports and things like that. We had so many exciting things to do we could never get them all done. It was thrilling. In fact I often wondered what kids did who didn't live on the desert.

Now, having traveled in various parts of the world, I know that fun is what you make it, anywhere. And there's nothing more fun than fun.

By the way, if you have to argue with the Lord about what you're planning to do, or where you're planning to go "for fun," you must be the one who is wrong in your direction. The Lord never is.

A boy once asked, "Mom! Is this shirt dirty?" What he meant, of course, was, "Do I have to change it?"

His mother was especially astute and she answered, "Son, if it's doubtful, it's dirty."

Have you ever thought of all the things a Christian can do that the average non-Christian never does? All kinds of church functions, youth rallies, Christian films, Christian parties, wonderful camps, among other things.

So many other fun activities are open to Christians also. Where to begin is the problem. Games that range from chess to golf. As for sports, we have swimming, boating, fishing, hiking, horseback riding, bike riding.

Recently I saw a sight that made me feel so good. There was a mother, with a little girl riding the basket of her bicycle. Dad had the baby with him. Two other children, about seven and ten I suppose, were riding along on their bikes.

There's skiing—summer and winter, sledding, tennis, volleyball, basketball, handball, softball, ping-pong, the possibilities are endless.

And music. What about the family "orchestra"? The fun a family can have practicing together. Maybe Mom at the piano or organ, Dad with his "fiddle"; son John with his guitar; sister following along on her uke. This family is wholly independent of "having to be entertained all the time." They're do-it-yourselfers. "Sing-a-long" is a word for the good old get-togethers. Families enjoy singing together. And what can be more uplifting.

Really, there's so much to do, so much fun right at our fingertips, that we'll never be able to do it all. But it's a lot of fun trying.

Practically all of this can be "family fun": time spent saying, "We love you. You're important to us. We would rather be with you than with anybody else in the whole world." "Love" isn't a term to be reserved exclusively for tennis!

Watch thirteen-year-old Phil hovering over his kid brother in the backyard, placing the younger kid's hands "just right" on the bat. Chances are that a few years back Phil learned the same way from his dad.

It's important, too, that mothers show an interest in the outdoor sports the boys are interested in. To be sure, the fellows may gripe, "Mom! You throw like a girl," but this is the mother a boy will talk with. "Since she's interested in my fun, then she's interested in me," he may reason. Mainly, he'll just accept this and grow a bit more secure all the time.

"Make the most of their wonder years," is the slogan of a well-known food product. We would do well to make it our family slogan.

It might seem sometimes that we're idly wasting time when we play at building sand castles with the children. The fact is that while the tide will come in and wash away our castles, it will never erase from the memory of a child, warm, loving thoughts of a father and mother who loved him enough to give this time.

We may well ask ourselves, "How could I better spend my leisure than in strengthening our family ties?"

It has been wisely said, "Tell me how a man spends his leisure hours, and I'll tell you what kind of a man he is." For the Christian, who will one day give an account to God, the family has a top priority until that time.

And some of it is for fun.

Chapter 10

PROGRAM'D TO DEATH

*And he [Jesus] said unto them, Come ye
yourselves apart into a desert place, and rest
a while: for there were many coming and
going.* Mark 6:31.

Junior high Judy dashes in from school. Half
out of breath she announces, "Mom! Don't fix
anything for me for supper. 4-H tonight, remember! Have to scoot and change. The kids'll
be here for me any minute." And Judy is off for
the Friday evening.

No sooner has she gone than her brother Dan
calls up from high school. "Sorry, Mother.
Should have told you we'd be working on the
props for the play again. Don't save supper. I'll
grab a hamburger at the corner. 'Bye now."

Beth Andrews surveys the table set for four.
She removes two places. She's frowning a bit.
This is happening too frequently.

In the Dalton home, things are reversed. Kathy comes home from school, a gleam in her eyes.

"Anybody home?" she sings out. No response. She tosses her books down and slumps onto the nearest chair. "Again!" she mutters. "Sometimes I wonder why I bother coming home at all. Oh, well," she eases up out of the chair, "Guess I'll go get something to eat and look for Mom's note." Sure enough, tucked under the edge of the fruit bowl on the dining room table was a note, "I'm sorry, Kathy, but this committee meeting of the Red Cross came up and I just had to go. Be a dear and start supper. Daddy has a board meeting tonight."

And so it goes. For Mother there is Red Cross, community drives for the Heart Fund, Cancer Crusade, Multiple Sclerosis, Cerebral Palsy and the Mothers' March for Birth Defects, volunteer work in the hospital and the League of Women Voters. Each activity worthy enough in itself. It's the combination that eats into home life.

As for Dad, he is chairman of the local Jay Cees, treasurer of the new library fund, secretary of his bowling league and a barbershopper to boot.

Likewise for the children no matter the age group there is multiplied activity: Boy and Girl Scouts, every kind of instruction from swimming to taking the German shepherd to obedience school. Home is rapidly becoming a place where members of the same family just run into each other enroute to some outside appointment.

And this is having a corroding effect on the Christian family. When, for instance, does everyone get together for worship? When do they sit down as a family and talk over the things that are important to all of them? Little happenings and big, material as well as spiritual.

For instance, this was the evening Kathy had hoped she could share a surprise with her mother and dad. Her science project had so impressed her teacher that he had called her in and said, "Keep this up, Kathy, and I'm reasonably sure we can work out a good scholarship for you for next year."

But Mother would rush in just before dinner, filled with her own committee stuff. Dad would gulp down dinner and be off to his board meeting. "They don't care. They're hardly ever home. We never talk together." And the bright science student had a hard time keeping back the tears.

Like Beth Andrews, Kathy had a feeling something was all wrong. Families should see more of each other than we ever do, she was thinking.

Do Mom and Dad get more out of being on committees and things like that than they do out of our being together? And Kathy had a frown on her face, too, as she pondered the question.

We might ask, shouldn't Christians become involved in community affairs? Is it right to expect that all the charitable fund-raising will be done by our non-Christian neighbors? And what about Bill Dalton with his training and skills—and his Christian viewpoint wouldn't he make a valuable contribution in his neighborhood? And our children! Are we going to deprive them of worthwhile activities with the children near by, when often their Christian friends are too far away to make friendship on a daily basis practical? These kinds of questions demand answers.

There is a sensible answer, of course. We do

owe certain loyalties to our community. We need to let our Christian voice be heard, especially where this has a direct bearing on our families.

A few years ago, the Department of Health in New York City proposed an ordinance that would have dealt a death blow to Vacation Bible Schools. Actually they had in mind day-care nurseries but the measures would have been broad enough to include VBS. Few churches would have met the board's standards as to space allotment, play facilities, trained workers and so on. The measure came to the attention of one pastor who spread the word by circular letter. The night of the hearing, the Board of Health members on the platform didn't know what had hit them. A nerve had been touched, and pastor and laymen crowded into the assigned room. Further hearings were called. The result? The matter was dropped. Christians had spoken up where it counted. This is one of the activities we need not consider poor stewardship of a Christian's time.

It's the pile up of activities which creates the problem. We need to be selective, especially while we still have young children and teenagers in our home.

This "rat race" is not confined to activities outside the church. Our churches are all too often guilty of "programming the members to death" as many a weekly bulletin will testify.

Gordon scans his church calendar as he waits for the morning service to begin. At the long line-up of meetings and activities he sighs. "Oh, for the good old days when church was the place we came to worship the Lord. Then we went out and put into practice what we learned the rest of

84

the week. And we got a midweek refill to keep going."

Ticking them off on his fingers, Gordon counted five activities/meetings that as a deacon of the church and a Sunday School teacher he would be expected to attend the coming week, not including Sunday! "If you want a job done, ask a man who's already busy," was the motto in this church, as Gordon had discovered. Of course, he may have to neglect his family, but he was serving his church.

Seven-year-old Peggy has a mother who is equally busy. She is a gifted Bible teacher and there's scarcely a day that she is not out at a meeting. Her husband's business keeps him away from home much of the time and more than one neighbor has invited the lonely little girl into her home. "Just look at that poor little thing, sitting on the curb playing with a stray cat, and her mother never home when she comes from school," one neighbor complained to another.

Years later Peggy's father asked his pastor, "Where did we fail our daughter?" You see she had just announced she was going to marry an avowed nonbeliever.

By contrast another equally acceptable teacher considered her home too important, and refused many an invitation while her children were still in the home. She had the pleasure of hearing her daughter say, "Mother, it's so nice when I step up to the front door. I can see right through to the kitchen and there you are."

Pastors' families notoriously suffer from a lack of parental attention and private family living.

Pastor Fraser's wife confided to another pastor's wife, "Maybe now that our oldest son has gotten into this awful trouble, his dad will believe me. I've tried to tell him that he's never home, and the boys talk about it. He's so busy fixing up other folks' families that he doesn't care if ours goes flat."

This can be equally true of any professional man. I well remember the telephone ringing three times one evening before we had hardly begun to eat dinner. A man was calling with a problem. I tried to suggest he see me the next day.

"Well, Dr. Narramore, aren't you going to help me?" he asked.

I said, "No, not right now."

He said, "Why not? Aren't you supposed to help people?"

I replied, "Yes, but I've already helped about five hundred people today. That's enough for one day." Then I asked him how old he was.

"Fifty," he told me.

"Well, you have lasted for fifty years. Do you think you can last one more day? I'll help you tomorrow."

Now that may sound hardhearted and I certainly am not in favor of that attitude. But there are times when we have to put the important task of meeting the needs of our own family above the demands of others. God has made us responsible for them. No one else can assume this responsibility. And I do not believe that the Lord is going to accept as an excuse, "But, Lord, you should have seen my schedule!"

Our children will either be a great blessing or a great tragedy to society and against the cause of Christ if we do not meet our obligation.

This calls for managing the schedule, not letting it manage us. It may mean taking the phone off the hook. It may even mean getting in the car and taking off for a little while.

A successful pastor in the Midwest has this plan that has worked for him and his family. Monday, right after school is family time for them. And indeed, before the children are out of school, he and his wife take time off together.

"We don't always do exciting things," this pastor explains. "Sometimes we sit and play a game of checkers, or whatever suits us at the moment. Or we talk over the sports of the day. Or do nothing in particular. But this is one evening when, as much as we possibly can, we're all home and interested in what each other is doing and thinking. We just shut out all the outside demands and have some time to ourselves."

Jesus used to do this with his disciples. They needed time to be alone, away from the pressures.

What is referred to as "the pressures of society" is certainly reflected in the Christian home. "Busy" has become a synonym for "godly" until the activity resembles and rivals a merry-go-round. Who is to say which of the church and church-related activities should be dispensed with. Missionary societies? A thousand times no! Pioneer girls, Boy's Christian Service Brigade, Child Evangelism, Christian Women's Club, Christian Businessmen's Committee? All worth while. All in the business of trying to win souls to Christ. And the list can go on.

But does everybody have to belong to everything? And how do we weed out the best-for-our-family from among the good things that beg for our time and interest?

Some families have found a council time pays off. At a planned time, the family gets together, each with a calendar and a pen or pencil. A chalkboard makes a fine addition as all the members can see it at once. Present obligations of each member of the family are listed, together with the amount of time entailed. The program then comes under discussion. In all of this the real end must be kept before each one, especially anyone who might resent having to give up some interest. The end? Closer family ties through time spent together and interest expressed in each other.

The Higgens, using the calendar planning, noticed that each of them was going to church on a different night all week. They talked this over with the pastor and Christian Education Director. Some other families had been conscious of the same problem. Sane discussion led to most of the family participation being planned for prayer meeting night. It became a family night in the church. This procedure saved evenings for the family. It saved either Mother or Dad doubling as a chauffeur night after night.

The Greens decided that since they all enjoyed bowling and each was bowling on different nights they would try an evening together. Even Grandpa went along and thoroughly enjoyed beating his son at the game.

The value of the calendar planning is reflected in much less frustration. There's far less, "I really must cut out something. I'm just too busy." Actually there's something in all of us that finds it difficult to resist, "Joe, our committee has discussed this, and you are the only man for the job.

We need you."

This seems much more important, much more ego building, according to some thinking than, "Goody! Daddy's home!" So we never practice saying, "No."

One of the finest Christian laymen I know is a man who doesn't show up every time the church door opens. He takes seriously the duties he has accepted as Sunday School superintendent, but by limiting his church obligations, he does a better job. And he has time to be a fine Christian husband and father.

Any member of the "calendar planning" family can most reasonably explain, "Well, I might think about this job, except our time is all accounted for now. You should see our family calendar!"

Obligations that are permitted to remain as scheduled are more important. The participant has more interest. A far cry from the "I'd better get this over with" attitude that an unrealistic schedule produces.

Above all, the home has a chance to become what God intended it should be. A place for the whole family to live for him, together. A place from which they might go, unharried, to witness for him. Not any one of even the best programs, or all of them put together, can ever take the place of a loving, warm home atmosphere. A wall sampler you may have seen describes the ideal Christian home:

"Where each lives for the other
And where all live for God."

This is the "program" that can be assured of having God's richest blessing.

Chapter 11

THE EXTRA MILE

Ye shall be witnesses unto me both in Jeru-
salem, and in all Judaea, and in Samaria,
and unto the uttermost part of the earth.
Acts 1:8.

Talking with the evangelist holding revival meetings in her church, a woman explained, "Dr. Jones, I feel God has something extra special for me to do. Would you please pray with me about this?"

"Ma'am," inquired the preacher, "do you have any children?"

"Oh, yes! The Lord has given us five wonderful children," she replied.

The preacher beamed at her. "There, my dear lady, is your 'extra special' assignment from the Lord."

The lady looked her disappointment. This wasn't what she had in mind, but with some wise counseling she understood and accepted her "Home Mission" assignment.

The Bible is never silent on these vital issues. Luke, the "beloved physician," recounts an interesting event. Among the many needy persons who inevitably gained the Saviour's attention was a demon-possessed man. In his miraculous way, the Lord delivered this man. Now if you had been he, what would you have wanted to do? Exactly! Jesus was getting into a boat and, Luke tells us: "The man from whom the demons had gone kept begging and praying that he might accompany Him and be with Him, but [Jesus] sent him away" (Luke 8:38, Amplified Bible).

What! Not become a disciple and be with Jesus and witness all the marvelous things he did! No! Jesus said, "Return to your home, and recount [the story].... And [the man] departed, proclaiming throughout the whole city how much Jesus had done for him" (verse 39).

And that's not the end of this story: "Now when Jesus came back [to Galilee], the crowd received and welcomed Him gladly, for they were all waiting and looking for Him" (verse 40).

All because a grateful individual obeyed the Lord and was faithful to his "hometown assignment."

Emily Maitland is a Sunday School teacher. One Sunday afternoon her teen-age daughter noticed that her mother looked depressed, not her usual cheery self.

"What's wrong, Mom?" Ruth inquired.

"Oh, honey, I think I should let somebody else take my class. I don't seem to be getting anywhere with them. Maybe the Lord can't use me."

"Mom! Don't you ever say that," her daughter interrupted, "remember you led me to the Lord."

Sometimes we hear snide remarks about "us four and no more." Well, it would seem that there's a sense in which we should make a concerted effort to win our own family first. This should in turn be the logical first step in the extra mile the Lord has bid us go.

We never know where this extra mile or extra step, taken for the Lord, will lead. There was Ed Kimball. Ask any of the folks who knew him at work. "Ed? He's a shoe clerk," they will tell you. But the Boston shoe salesman realized that making a living wasn't the greatest contribution he could make. Ed was a Sunday School teacher and in his class of boys was a young fellow to whom Ed witnessed faithfully. He visited the lad in his home and talked to him about his soul. Came the day when young Dwight L. Moody surrendered his heart and life to Christ. No, Ed Kimball couldn't have imagined that this boy would shake two continents for God. That a great Bible institute bearing his name would send forth Bible-taught servants to the ends of the earth. Ed was simply sharing his faith.

So was Miss Barkely, Steve Landon's English teacher. At eighteen Steve was one of the roughest, toughest football players that ever hit Washington High—all six foot two and 195 pounds of him.

"How does that kid ever stay in school?" folks asked. "He breaks every rule in the book!"

The climax came one Monday morning. Steve had been drinking the night before, then, after a big fight at home he stumbled to school ready to "whip the world."

Miss Barkely had always taken an interest in Steve and she greeted him this Monday morning as he appeared in the library. Sensing the boy was in serious trouble, she followed him to his locker.

"It's no use talking to me," he snapped at the teacher. "I've got my own life to live and I'm going to live it just the way I please."

All that day Miss Barkely kept praying for Steve. "They'll expel him this time, for sure," she said to herself. That evening she called him and asked him to come over to her house. Figuring, "If ever I needed a friend, it's now," Steve took his teacher up on her invitation.

Not only did she tell Steve about Christ, what he could do for a young fellow who would trust him, the real happiness he could know; but she also persuaded him to accompany her a few nights later to a crusade in the city auditorium.

Slouched down in his seat in the very last row, Steve listened to the powerful gospel preaching. At the end of the service he headed for the altar.

"I couldn't get there fast enough," he admitted, "and when a counselor talked to me, right there and then I decided to settle the whole thing. I told God that from now on, I wanted to live for him—and I never meant anything so seriously in my whole life."

Miss Barkeley helped to have Steve reinstated in school. He went on to graduate, then college, and before long Steve became an outstanding youth leader in his area. And he never tires of telling of his high school teacher who talked with him, befriended him, prayed and counseled with him until he came to know Christ as his Saviour.

Sometimes it's the other way around: the pupil witnessing to the teacher. Wendy was just a second grader. She came skipping home one day, her face radiant: "Mommie," she burst out the minute she got in the door, "my teacher is a Christian!"

"Oh, tell me about it," her mother encouraged the little girl.

"Well, Mommie, you know Daddy and you have always said we should tell other people about Jesus and I didn't know if anybody had ever told Miss Brown. So just before recess, I bowed my head a little bit and I prayed that I wouldn't be afraid to ask her if she knows Jesus as her Saviour. And Mommie, I prayed Jesus wouldn't let her be mad at me."

Now as it happened, Wendy's teacher does know Jesus. But imagine her delight that one of her own pupils cared enough to witness to her. And would not this send her out to "do likewise"?

Jack Wyrtzen is another who can thank God today for the faithful witness of an army buddy, George Schilling. They had been fellow trombone players in a jazz band before George came to know Christ.

George's conversion was a revelation to Jack. When they were shipped off to an army camp together, Jack was quite certain George's "religion" would never stand up. Not in this tough army crowd!

Jack watched his friend like a hawk, night and day. He was driven to the conclusion that "George has something worth having."

Still, despite all of George's consistent Christian life, and the testimony of God's Word as

George shared it with him, Jack was not ready to give his life to Christ.

It was after he had played his trombone at an evangelistic service where he sat completely miserable under the preaching of the gospel, that Jack Wyrtzen went home and alone in his room, he knelt and received Christ into his heart and life.

The years have passed and through his personal preaching and on radio, many thousands have come to know Christ. The Lord led Jack to establish Christian camps, both in the United States and in a number of foreign countries, where countless persons of all ages have been blessed through the gospel ministry.

George Schilling could undoubtedly have used his time in other ways, but he realized it was his business, as Peter tells us, to "be ready always to give an answer to every man that asketh you a reason of the hope that is in you" (I Peter 3:15).

A woman asked her bread salesman, "Young man, are you a Christian?"

Her daughter-in-law, horrified, exclaimed, "Why, Mother, that's none of your business!"

"Oh, yes it is my business," the older woman quickly answered, and she promptly invited the young man to her home for Sunday supper. He accepted, went with the family to church that evening, and alone in his room late that night he accepted Christ as his Saviour.

This man, too, has become a powerful preacher giving out "the bread of life." All possible because one woman shared her faith, and went the extra mile to help save a soul.

Have you ever tried to witness to someone and been asked, "What's in it for you?" It seems we're so conditioned in our society that we suspect something unselfish. "Must be a catch in it" or the person making the offer "has an angle."

We might shrink from the thought of witnessing for Christ with anything less than a pure motive but it's worth considering just the same.

Young Tommy has no scruples when he invites a friend up the street to come to Sunday School with him.

"We're having a contest, see! And if you'll come with me, I'll get points for a prize."

Are we ever guilty of trying to win someone "for points"?

John and Christine had been friends for a long time. They were practically engaged. Then something happened and they broke off the friendship. Some months later, John came to know Christ. Almost immediately he got in touch with Christine, made a date to talk with her about "the wonderful thing that's happened to me."

Telling of this experience later, Christine freely admitted, "It was the fact that he didn't try to persuade me to go back with him. Not at all. All he wanted to talk about was God and how much difference it makes when you know Christ. It all sounded so good, like something I had wanted all my life. Johnny was so sincere about it. I'll never be able to thank him enough for sharing it with me."

Oh, yes! They got together, Johnny and Christine, and for these more than twelve years, they and their children have served the Lord together in South America.

Had John been "looking for points" chances are he never would have won Christine to the

Lord. "It was his concern for my soul," said Christine, "that so impressed me."

Frank Graham came to his pastor one day with a problem. "Pastor Brown," he began, "I wish you'd pray with Phyllis and me about my dad. You know he lives with us, and do we have problems! He smokes, and this keeps Phyllis up in the air most of the time. She complains that he smells up the whole house. And it's true. Things like this are about wrecking our marriage and I thought—well, if Dad would get saved, that would solve a lot of problems for us."

Undoubtedly, salvation would work changes in the elder Mr. Graham. But is this couple one little bit concerned about the father's soul? The fact that here is an elderly man facing eternity without Christ, has this struck Frank and Phyllis? It would appear from Frank's own admission that the real motive is a desire for a more comfortable home situation for themselves.

Then there's people like Sarah Adams. Sarah was quick to tell of how many persons she had witnessed to and how many had accepted Christ through her efforts. One Sunday morning, she talked with another woman who responded to the pastor's invitation. Later she took the woman to the pastor and, most insistently, urged her to tell the pastor how she had helped her. Her motive stuck out all over. Self glory.

When all has been said on the subject of "the extra mile" it boils down to this: As God's witnesses we have a clear-cut duty to share the Good News of the Gospel. We are not to treat it as some kind of highly classified secret data. If we do not know how, we have a duty to find out and your pastor will be delighted to instruct you.

Also, there are many fine books written on the subject of soulwinning. A visit to a Christian bookstore will convince you of this.

There is nothing to be compared with this kind of sharing. It gives a glow inside that not the gloomiest day or most adverse circumstance can dim.

And who knows? Maybe the very next person you lead to Christ will become another Dwight L. Moody, or a Paul Carlson. Surely it's worth that "extra mile"! And "he that winneth souls is wise" (Proverbs 11:30). "And they that be wise shall shine as the brightness of the firmament; and they that turn many to righteousness as the stars for ever and ever" (Daniel 12:3).

Chapter 12

THE HOUSE DIVIDED

*He said to me, My grace—My favor and lov-
ing-kindness and mercy—are enough for you
. . . to enable you to bear the trouble [man-
fully]; for My strength and power are made
perfect . . . show themselves most effective—
in [your] weakness.*

II Corinthians 12:9, Amplified Bible.

Who would deny that in our day one of the
greatest of human problems that many have to
face is the tragedy of being left alone to care for
a family. For whatever the reason, a one-parent
home is always a calamity to a greater or lesser
degree.

Although the following letter points up the
problems a sole mother faces, similar concerns
are expressed by sole fathers who write us.

Dear Dr. Narramore:
I lost my husband several years ago, and I am
raising my three sons—two of them teenagers—
alone. I want very much to keep my children in

school long enough so that they can be educated and be able to care for themselves when they're grown. By selling the car I'm keeping expenses down so I can save a little for this. I do not work outside my home as I like to be here available to my children when needed. I see too much of children of working mothers coming home to an empty house. It isn't good.

I would like any suggestions you may have on how to raise boys without a father or husband in the home.

This is a question I'm asked very often. "What can you do, as a woman, raising these boys so they'll grow up to the best advantage?"

First let me encourage you with this fact: many well adjusted people who have made contributions to society are the products of a one-parent home. Life offers many problems and the sole parent undoubtedly faces more than his share.

I think of my own mother, widowed when she was in her forties, a pioneer woman living on a western ranch. Her life was not an easy one but she knew Christ as her Saviour and friend. Trusting him for guidance, she devoted herself to raising her seven children. Looking back now, I understand the secret of the calm and triumphant spirit that made her life an inspiration to everybody who knew her. As a boy I often looked into her room and saw her kneeling beside her bed, talking with her Saviour. Mother read her Bible and walked with God.

So what would be my advice to the writer of this letter we quoted?

Surrender to Christ daily. God knows and cares for you. The Lord is your greatest resource, and when your children see you leaning hard on him, they will begin to do the same.

Face your situation realistically. Since problems are never solved by denying they exist, it is useless to attempt to either ignore or hide the fact that you are a single parent. Being realistic and honest with yourself is one of the first marks of maturity.

Don't try to be a man. Some mothers, in order to compensate for the lack of a husband, try to enact the part of both a mother and a father. This is not possible, nor is it necessary.

Spend time with your children. I was pleased to note the wisdom of the writer of the letter in this respect. She knew the value of being home with her children. You'll recall the incident in an earlier chapter of the little fellow who said, "My daddy loves me. I know it, because he plays with me."

Spending time with your children has other advantages: this is how you will learn to understand them. Their strengths and weaknesses, interests, abilities, fears, worries.

And what you are "rubs off" on the child, as you communicate with each other. Since he has only you to turn to, it's important that you be approachable and understanding. This will keep the lines of communication open, and by talking about what he feels, your child will be able to think through his own problems.

Don't "mother" to the point of s-mother-ing. Emphasize self-reliance. It's not showing love to shield a child from responsibility. This may meet a need in the mother's life but prevents the child from growing and developing into the poised confident person he is capable of becoming.

Encourage friendships with other children and for the boys, be sure to arrange male associations. A man teacher in school or Sunday School can be most helpful.

Stress salvation and spiritual growth. This is the ultimate advice. The most important thing in life is to be saved and to live a dynamic Christian life. Start early to lead your child in the ways of the Lord.

"You have a great responsibility and privilege in raising these three boys," I would tell the mother who wrote me.

Now we are well aware that there are multitudes of solo-parent homes caused by divorce or separation of the parents. In raising the children, the same principles would apply. I would add, however, don't blame your troubles on your former mate. This brings no solution. Remember, a child is not especially interested in whether his father was right, or his mother. What interests him is the present. Not who's to blame for the past.

For the solo parents, there are in some communities what is called a "Solo Parents Club." Attending this can be helpful as persons involved with the situation share experiences.

Another area of family concern that floods the mailbox in our Counseling Clinic is the matter of "the extra person": relatives, in-laws. These letters don't tell about folks like Bobby's grandpa. This grandfather lives with Bobby and his parents. Grandpa is a top-flight-fix-it man. To quote his grandson, "My grandpa can fix anything. Nobody knows as much as Grandpa." Here is an in-law who is making a great contribution in the family.

Then there's Aunt Mary who lives with her in-laws. Not such a fixer as Bobby's grandpa, but a teacher. Oh, Aunt Mary doesn't hold classes. But she has been a school teacher. She's also traveled a great deal throughout the world. She loves to tell her interesting experiences and show beautiful pictures and fascinating souvenirs. In fact, this family would have missed out a great deal of enrichment in their lives, if Aunt Mary hadn't come to live with her sister.

The other side of the coin comes through in our mail: the frustration of lost privacy, the demands made by relatives. Here are just a sample of these:

"Aunt Sylvia refuses to eat toast unless she butters it herself."

"Cousin Jake can't go to bed until he's heard the 10:45 news. No other newscast will do."

"Grandma Archer always expects to sit in the front seat of the car. 'It's more comfortable,' she says."

People who must be pampered become problems.

So, for the relative who contemplates or already is living-in with some of the family, eliminating a demanding attitude will bring dividends.

Grandma and Grandpa Swanson were loved by every member of the family with whom they lived. They had learned some important "how-to's": On occasions they would "waive" an invitation to "Come, join us. The Graham's have just dropped in for coffee. Don't go off to bed yet, Grandma and Grandpa." Wisely, they realized the family needed time by themselves, and with their company.

Then, too, Grandpa would say to his son, "Jim, my boy, you know how to pick a winner. Barbara's as sweet as she's pretty. And her pies!" And Grandma would nod and smile in complete agreement. Not flattery but a genuine compliment is what the Bible calls, "A word fitly spoken . . . like apples of gold in pictures of silver."

Another battleground with in-laws in particular is interfering with the children. Most parents feel that their children are their very personal responsibility and not to be tampered with by others. So if you want to be successful with the family with whom you live, don't forget to keep "hands off" in the discipline of the children. And no dire predictions regarding the teenagers in the home.

Speaking of teenagers, Dr. Billy Graham said, "I think teenagers are great. Today's teenagers are the finest generation in history. More informed, more idealistic, more religiously inclined. They're not in revolt against God and Christ. They're in revolt against the caricature of the church they see."

Some have said to their parents, "If you would only try to see us as we are, instead of trying to fit us into your generation."

If you did "see him as he is," what would you see? Possibly what Gilbert and Sullivan would refer to as "a most amazing paradox."

One minute Jim amazes his folks with his knowledge of world affairs. The next fifteen minutes they look out and see him hanging by his toes from the limb of a tree. Jim seemed to be a man of the world one minute, a boy the next. Parents and teachers should face the fact of Jim's unpredictability and encourage rather than condemn, be patient rather than irritable.

Bonnie complained, "Mother treats me as a child when it's something I want to do, and like an adult when it's something she wants me to do!"

Intellectually as well as physically the teenager is rapidly developing. His mental powers, reaching maturity, cry out for challenges and for solid, adult answers. Teenagers may demand proof. The simple answers given them earlier may no longer suffice.

What we said earlier will bear repeating: "A teenager is a bundle of possibilities." When we work with them we can't dream to what heights one of them may climb. A president? A brain surgeon? A world leader? A missionary?

As Billy Graham said, "A teenager is an idealist." What better time than now—when heroes are in his thinking—to point him to the one who "is altogether lovely," "the chiefest among ten thousand" (Song of Solomon 5:10,16).

A teenager is capable but short on experience. Most of them are ready to tackle anything. But not yet have they learned the value of experience. Nor are they always ready to listen to the advice of someone who has!

When Jack started out from Camp Maple Bay to row a boat load of girls across the inlet, he was capable. He could handle a boat. In fact Jack was one of the finest athletes in camp.

What Jack didn't know was that at certain times and with certain tides there was a strong current. Row as he might, Jack soon found himself in difficulties drifting out into the bay! His strength was exhausted, and nothing ever looked so good to him as the motor boat sent out by the camp director. Here was experience in such matters ready to tow them all back.

As parents and teachers we can help young people in the stream of life, but we should be tactful and patient so that they will profit by our experience.

A teenager has a passion for popularity. To do and be what their "peer group" do and are, this is the thing. How vital then that we do everything we possibly can to put our Christian young people in contact with others who love the Lord.

The teenager analyzes himself in the eyes of others. In fact he is often much more concerned with what others think of him than of his own self-evaluation. It was an adult Polonius who said:

"This above all, to thine own self be true,
And it must follow, as night the day,
That thou canst not then
Be false to any man."

But we can bring to a teenager's mind that it was a teen-age Daniel, a student, who "Purposed in his heart that he would not defile [conform] himself with . . . the king's meat, nor . . . wine" (Daniel 1:8). It was three other young Jewish fellows who dared to be different; dared to defy the king's decree even if it meant a fiery death. (See Daniel 3:18.) And these four made a place in history!

Teenagers are bundles of energy. Mrs. Douglas just couldn't figure out her son. He would stick faithfully at his homework until around 9:00 every night, then he'd disappear. He wasn't gone long enough for a milk shake, or to meet anybody. He would come puffing in within fifteen minutes and settle back to work. Finally she just had to find out.

"George, where do you go when you take off like that?"

"Oh, I just take a run around the block, Mom. The air feels so good."

Another thing that bears repeating about teenagers is that, in spite of all we hear to the contrary, they prefer some rules and regulations.

Joan's mother gave her daughter complete liberty and was apt to brag of Joan's good sense. "I would never dream of setting an hour when she must be home!"

But Joan didn't feel this way. She sought out an older woman, a friend of her mother's, to talk over her problem.

"I don't think Mother really loves me," she lamented, "she doesn't care what time I come in. I wish she would set an hour, or lay down some rules!"

The teenager needs so many things. He needs our love, even if he's too shy to reciprocate; our pride, even if he often fails; our encouragement when things go against him; our confidence when his own is lacking. Above all, he needs God. He needs to look up and say, "My father, thou art the guide of my youth" (Jeremiah 3:4).

Problems of "solo parents," in-laws, teenagers, all have their true solution in the God of the Bible. He assures us, "My grace is sufficient for thee" (II Corinthians 12:9). Sufficient for successful Christian family living.

Chapter 13

CONSOLIDATING OUR GAINS

This book of the law shall not depart out of thy mouth; but thou shalt meditate therein day and night, that thou mayest observe to do according to all that is written therein: ... and then thou shalt have good success.
Joshua 1:8.

We've come to the final chapter in this book, and maybe we are about ready to pose a few questions:

1. Does God's "Success Plan" apply today?

2. What are the top priority areas for a change-for-the-better in my family?

3. What changes will this mean for me?

Since we're practical people, it makes sense to ask, "Does it work?"

People write books and give lectures on how to be successful. Yet, so often they leave out the basic element. Real success cannot be achieved anywhere but in the center of God's will.

Bill is a good example of what happens when we are in partnership with God. Bill had struggled along, making little if any headway. Then one day he met a fellow who encouraged him to come to church.

"Why not?" Bill thought, "I've tried everything else."

He came, was intensely interested, and in the course of an evangelistic campaign some weeks later, Bill received Christ as his personal Saviour.

Bill began to study the Bible with his new-found Christian friends. He grew in the Lord and became a changed fellow. Everything seemed different. And it was.

His job? Actually, his job remained the same, but his attitude was different. Now Bill was working for and with Jesus, his Lord and Saviour.

A few years later Bill was transferred to the Pacific Northwest, working for the same company—but he was also working for God. He bought a bus and on Sundays he filled it with children from rural areas and brought them to church and to Sunday School. He started an active home missionary project, working evenings, Sundays and during vacations.

Now Bill is one of the most successful men in the world. And it all began when he went into partnership with God.

I knew a teen-age girl named Gloria. She was vivacious and pretty, and her ambition in life was to become an actress and star in the theater.

"Oh, Dr. Narramore!" she sighed, "I can't think of anything more fabulous than to be a movie star. I do hope I have enough talent. It's so—so glamorous."

We talked for a little while. She listened intently as I told her about the Lord Jesus Christ and what he wanted her to do with her life. No! She didn't accept him right then and there, but it wasn't long until she did.

I saw Gloria again a few months later. She was a different person, a new creature. I asked her, "What about your Hollywood career, Gloria?"

"Oh, Dr. Narramore," she said, "stop kidding me. I haven't the least desire in the world to be in show business. I want to serve the Lord."

And she did—and is still.

Following high school and Bible college, Gloria went with her handsome husband to work as a staff musician on a foreign missionary radio station. Here she is working in a job where her talents really lie. Gloria, too, has achieved success in God's plan.

It works, as it always has. Even in our space age. Our space age bears several trademarks. One of these is insecurity. People want to be secure in every realm of life, but the most important security is often overlooked. Only in recent years have psychologists and psychiatrists begun to analyze man with a new dimension in mind. This new dimension: FAITH. "Faith in a Supreme Being," they're saying, "brings stability and security."

We're presuming that at this point, you, the reader, are aware that salvation is by faith. That you have received the gift of God, eternal life, through faith in his Son Jesus Christ, and that now we can move into what we might call "working faith." (See James 2:18.)

"Show and tell" is an integral part of early education in our schools. This same "show and tell" faith in action is where the home comes in. It's in the home we can implement what we've been considering in these chapters.

This brings us to our second question as it relates to changes for the better in our family.

Have our family devotions been hit and miss?

Has just about anything been justification for postponing or canceling our family worship?

One change might be, resolving to let the phone ring rather than allowing the answering of it to break up the worship together. And folks who pop in at this time? Shall we graciously explain and invite them to join us?

As for our children and teenagers, we will ask God to burn into our minds what is ths long-range effect on each one of them, of the right attitudes they can sense in our home. We'll not be content only with formal worship—reading the Bible and praying together. We'll honestly seek to make "pleasing God" a way of life. And, as parents, we'll lead the way, always with love.

Another change may be the revising or revolutionizing of our schedule of activities; the weeding out the best from the good and "gooder," in order to spend more time with our children while they need us.

And we'll not only tell them and each other that we love them, but also we'll show it by the way we act—by thoughtfulness expressed in action.

And maybe we will want to make some changes in the magazine subscriptions we have, exchange some for more worthwhile *Christian periodicals*. And the record cabinet? Could it do with a few subtractions and additions?

Then, too, this somewhat in-depth coverage of

114

the subject of successful family living may have shown us "discipline" in a new light. As something we do for and with our children, not to them. Knowledge that will make "Do's and Don'ts" more reasonable when we have to enforce them. This in contrast with former inflexible arbitrary rules that often bred resentment rather than having "training" value.

We will have failed in the overall purpose of this book if we haven't motivated you to go the "extra mile." Investing ourselves in others, this has been called. It's the one investment we need never doubt will pay off.

"But I can't go into all the world," you may be excusing yourself. Right! Nobody can. But there is a point on the compass that everybody can reach. It's not north, or south, or east, or west. It's right where you are. First, in your "Jerusalem" (home). From there you can branch out to the neighbors. Seeing the woman next door as your spiritual responsibility before God—not just as someone to enjoy a cup of coffee and a chat with.

We've said nothing about finances up to now, but we can never go that extra mile into "all the world" without giving God his rightful share. Giving "as God hath prospered him" (I Corinthians 16:2).

The devil would tempt us to rationalize about our giving. This happened to Paul and Louise. They regularly met their monthly expenses, but suddenly an emergency confronted them. For as long as they had been Christians, they had tithed their income. God had always blessed them, but now. . . .

"Honey, I know what," Paul suggested, "if we

skip our tithe we can meet our bills. We can make it up afterwards."

"No, Paul," Louise answered, shaking her head. "That wouldn't be right. Our tithe belongs to the Lord. I believe if we honor God and give our tithe as we always have, somehow the Lord will see us through this financial struggle."

Paul thought a moment. Then stepping over and placing a kiss on his wife's forehead, he agreed, "You're right, dear. I'm glad you feel this way about it. We'll give our tithe as usual and we'll trust the Lord to meet our need." And God did.

It always pays to be obedient to God.

Question number three, "What changes will this mean for me?" might probe a little deeper under the skin.

As you've read some of the illustrations of how God has worked in another's life you've felt a response in your own heart: "That sounds just like me, I could do that. That's exactly what we need in our home." And not only the Holy Spirit, but also your own innate honesty tells you, "I have to do something about it."

Maybe it's, "I'll have to discipline myself to get up a half hour earlier in the morning to insure my quiet time with God in preparation for all the day will bring."

"A forgiving spirit," one woman wrote. "If I could only have a forgiving spirit. I say I forgive, but I can't forget. I'm afraid this isn't real forgiveness."

This lady is right. Suppose the Lord forgave but never forgot? "I, even I, am he that blotteth out thy transgressions . . . and will not remember thy sins" (Isaiah 43:25).

How many, men and women alike, are like the Indian who admitted, "I bury the hatchet, but I always leave the handle sticking up."

It's a good resolution, then, to ask God for the special grace to forgive and forget!

You may want to turn back to the first chapter and with some new insights gained from the written experiences of other people like yourself, completely re-evaluate yourself.

And here's a word for you when you have decided on some changes you have to make. Do it now. It may call for some humbling. That won't be one bit easier tomorrow, believe me.

If making less than the maximum use of your time has been your problem, and you're asking the Lord to help you "redeem the time," this will call for some cooperation with the Lord. It will take will power and self-discipline. God isn't going to turn off the TV. He is not going to close the book you're reading and put it away when you know you should be busy tidying up the house or getting dinner.

Come to think of it, remember "Fred and the screen door" incident from Chapter 4? Suppose Fred could have gotten at the job and fixed that door, if he'd been willing to give up something he would rather do? It would have prevented an emotional scene in his home. And nothing is more worthwhile than this: preserving a happy atmosphere.

And, father, maybe you have decided to look squarely at this matter of being the God-ordained head of the house, responsible to God in this capacity. You hadn't really given it much thought before, but since it's all that important, you're going to have to make a few changes.

117

Take the children to Sunday School, for instance, instead of dropping them and their mother off and coming back just in time for church!

Prayer meeting, too. We're not camels that can store up enough nourishment to last from one Sunday to the next.

"If I could only have the opportunity to start over," oh, how often we hear this. Well it may be that right now, with honest facing up to what may have been problems or shortcomings in the past, your family has that chance for a new start. All kinds of helps are available to parents these days—spiritual and psychological.

Every sincere child of God can be a success—should be a success.

Every home where mother and dad are real born-again believers, anxious to please God, can know the satisfaction of "successful family living."

For when God is in charge there can be no failure.

In the final analysis, it's faith all the way. Trust the Lord. Put firm confidence in his Word, know from practical experience the meaning of the apostle Paul's words: "I can do all things through Christ which strengtheneth me" (Philippians 4:13).

What a wonderful thought—to know that as believers we have this special, supernatural help to make us successful.

That's what it will take to make your home successful—the supernatural. Joshua gives us the unfailing formula, the Bible's "How to do it." "This book of the law shall not depart out of thy mouth; but thou shalt meditate therein day and night, that thou mayest observe to do according

118

to all that is written therein: for then thou shalt make thy way prosperous, and then thou shalt have good success" (Joshua 1:8).

Doesn't this make you kind of anxious to get at it? To proceed with your personal experiment in "How to Succeed in Family Living" God's way?